Comprehending

PROBLEM SOLVING

Comprehending

PROBLEM | SOLVING

Building Mathematical Understanding with Cognition and Language

ARTHUR HYDE

Foreword by **Ellin Oliver Keene**

HEINEMANN
Portsmouth, NH

Heinemann
361 Hanover Street
Portsmouth, NH 03801–3912
www.heinemann.com

Offices and agents throughout the world

The author and publisher wish to thank those who have generously given permission to reprint borrowed material:

Excerpts from Common Core State Standards © Copyright 2010. National Governors Association Center for Best Practices and Council of Chief State School Officers. All rights reserved.

NRC excerpts adapted from "Strands of Mathematical Proficiency" in *Adding It Up: Helping Children Learn Mathematics* by the National Research Council, Mathematics Learning Study Committee, and Jeremy Kilpatrick, Jane Swafford, and Bradford Findell, editors. Copyright © 2001 by the National Academy of Sciences. Reprinted by permission of National Academy Press conveyed via Copyright Clearance Center.

Excerpts adapted from "An Emerging Model of the Language of Mathematics" by Sue Gawned in *Language in Mathematics* edited by Jennie Bickmore-Brand. Copyright © 1990 by Australian Reading Association. Distributed in North America by Heinemann, Portsmouth, NH. All rights reserved.

Figures 3.3 and 5.3 from *Understanding Middle School Math: Cool Problems to Get Students Thinking and Connecting* by Arthur Hyde. Copyright © 2009 by Arthur Hyde. Published by Heinemann, Portsmouth, NH. All rights reserved.

Library of Congress Cataloging-in-Publication Data
Hyde, Arthur A.
  Comprehending problem solving : building mathematical understanding with cognition and language / Arthur Hyde ; foreword by Ellin Oliver Keene.
      pages cm
  Includes bibliographical references.
  ISBN: 978-0-325-04924-3
  1. Mathematics—Study and teaching (Elementary)—Handbooks, manuals, etc. 2. Elementary school teachers—Training of—Handbooks, manuals, etc. 3. Mathematics teachers—Training of—Handbooks, manuals, etc. I. Title.
QA135.6.H915 2015
372.7—dc23   2014024939

Editor: Katherine Bryant
Production: Victoria Merecki
Cover design: Suzanne Heiser
Cover image: © ULKASTUDIO/Shutterstock
Interior design: Shawn Girsberger
Typesetter: Shawn Girsberger
Manufacturing: Steve Bernier

Printed in the United States of America on acid-free paper
18   17   16   15   14   VP   1   2   3   4   5

Contents

With contributions from:

Deanna Bero, Wheaton School District, IL
Megan Bostrom, Wheaton School District, IL
Sara Garner, Wheaton School District, IL
Becky Hanselman, Wheaton School District, IL
Susan Hildebrand, Jenks, OK
Christina Hull, Wheaton School District, IL
Loretta Johnson, Barrington School District, IL
Julie Kanturek, Marquardt School District, IL
Stephanie Krizmis, Schaumburg School District, IL
Laura Meehan, Barrington School District, IL
Pam Regan, River Forest School District, IL
Jennifer Schramm, Hinsdale School District, IL
Amy Tepavchevich, Naperville School District, IL
Alice Valencia, Wheeling School District, IL
Emily Wiegand, Westchester School District, IL

Foreword

THIS IS THE SECOND TIME I've been privileged to write a foreword for the incomparable Art Hyde. He's a math guy. I'm a literacy person. Yet I've just read a *whole math book* and was completely engaged throughout. When I mention this to my family and friends, I'm met with peals of laughter. "You can't even change a percentage to a decimal." More laughter. My dad reminds me of my "epic problems with long division." Aren't I fortunate to have such a sweet and supportive group around me?! But as Art says, "Language is the quintessential human attribute," and on that point we share tremendous passion and conviction.

I'm inspired and intrigued by Art's work because at its core is using language to understand math concepts. He describes the braid model of problem solving "in which cognition, language, and mathematics are woven together very intentionally so that students can develop significant understanding." In *Comprehending Problem Solving*, he clearly describes how cognitive processes I've so often taught in reading and writing pertain to math learning.

Most teachers with whom I work juggle maintaining an active, engaging classroom environment, addressing Common Core State Standards, and preparing children for assessments. As a response to the overwhelming amount of curriculum, teachers are often advised to integrate subject areas. In this book, Art goes beyond the lip service given to integration by showing how the disciplines are connected not by themes but by thinking processes. He argues that if we're talking to children about using prior knowledge to build understanding as they read, for example, we should use the same language to help children understand math.

Comprehending Problem Solving has even changed my thinking about mathematical concepts I thought I understood. I understood, for example, that engaging students in problem-solving activities and asking them to use language to explain their reasoning is a useful way for them to "show what they know." But Art broadens our ideas about problem solving: "Attacking good problems is not an application of what students have already learned; it is the major vehicle for building new meaning." The practical and research-based practices he promotes make me want to dive in and be a part of math teaching and learning all over again.

I was particularly drawn to Chapter 4. In it, Art shows how even very young children can create mathematical models. "Students are expected to bring their own personal meaning to bear on a problem and to test and revise their interpretation as they grapple with the problem situation." Maybe it was the chocolate algebra example that made so much sense, but I was able to see exactly how children can develop a viable model to explain math problems. The likelihood that they will retain and reapply these concepts seems high. They are fully engaged in *creating* models others can use to understand math concepts.

We are drawn into dozens of classroom experiences through Art's collaboration with math teachers in Illinois and Oklahoma. Megan, a first-grade teacher, describes how Luke exceeded most adults' expectations to think abstractly. Amy, who moved from intermediate to primary grades, describes her surprise when her young students are able to engage in sophisticated mathematical discourse. Instructional coaches Loretta and Laura describe how they use reading strategies (I've heard of those!) to help third graders understand the abstract concept of planetary speed around the sun. These vignettes bring so much clarity and life to the pages of this book; I could see the children they describe popping out of their seats to propose a theory, based on their work with Unifix cubes, for finding a way to put horses in a corral.

Finally, I want to mention Art's contribution to our thinking about planning math instruction. He does not provide scripts and prescriptions for teachers to follow, in his words, "slavishly." He trusts teachers to mull over a number of "considerations" as we plan. The considerations are a set of questions that remind us what matters most in planning to teach math (or any other subject, in my view). Planning around these considerations (essential concepts, big ideas, authentic experiences, metacognition, grouping structures, etc.) allows teachers to provide the most authentic and engaging math experiences possible—to put the great ideas in this book into practice. I deeply appreciate an author whose respect for teachers is represented by his refusal to prescribe the way teachers plan their instruction and interact with their students.

In fact, I deeply appreciate Art Hyde. In his extraordinarily distinguished career, he has brought math into the light for thousands and thousands of teachers and children. He has helped those of us who considered ourselves math-phobic to shed the fear and even shame that came from our background of very inauthentic math instruction and embrace mathematical thinking as readily as we have embraced reading well-loved literature and writing the stories of our lives. Art's way of looking at math is for all of us and for all our children.

—*Ellin Oliver Keene*

Introduction

What humans do with the language of mathematics is to describe patterns. Mathematics is an exploratory science that seeks to understand every kind of pattern—patterns that occur in nature, patterns invented by the human mind, and even patterns created by other patterns. To grow mathematically, children must be exposed to a rich variety appropriate to their own lives through which the can see variety, regularity, and interconnections.

—Lynn Arthur Steen (1990)

I HAVE BEEN TEACHING MATHEMATICS to students and teachers for more than thirty years. Consequently, I have formed some strong opinions about what mathematics is and how we should teach it. For many of these opinions, there is now substantial support from research in mathematics education and cognitive psychology. The support that I value most highly comes from teachers who have tried my ideas in their own practice.

In a brief overview I want to introduce you to the way I think about my own teaching of math, how I plan for it, and what I emphasize. In the subsequent chapters I will elaborate on these ideas and provide some examples of activities I have done with students in their schools. I also will include activities that I have asked teachers to write for this book.

Teaching Mathematics

Three ideas have been at the heart of my work with students and teachers: (1) mathematics is the science of patterns; (2) the goal of our teaching is helping students to *understand* and that will take a lot of work in cognition; (3) communication about mathematics and human cognition is done with language.

Mathematics Is the Science of Patterns

In many ways mathematical concepts are patterns, relationships among ideas. Patterns are found in every branch of school mathematics. They include *number* concepts in arithmetic such as prime numbers, subtraction, and logarithms; *algebraic* concepts such as variable, expression, and coefficient; *geometric* concepts such as length, area, volume, symmetry, and similarity; *measurement* concepts with both metric and traditional English units; *data* concepts, which are often called *numbers* in a context; and *probability* concepts such as chance, random, odds, outcomes.

The goal of teaching and learning mathematics is for students to *understand* these concepts and patterns, not merely commit to memory a cacophony of facts and procedures. We want students to understand how facts fit together and why procedures work. Because understanding is the goal, teachers, curriculum developers, and assessment specialists *must* attend to what we have learned from the cognitive sciences about the nature of understanding and how to help students achieve it.

Conceptual Understanding

Concepts in mathematics are abstract relationships among objects, actions, and ideas. Students understand a concept when they have developed a generalized sense of how the concept applies to a wide range of contexts and they can represent the concept in multiple ways. For example, students often get confused when confronted with the multiple meanings of the concept of subtraction. It can mean *comparison* or *difference* as well as the more familiar *take away*. Despite the fact that as a verb *subtract* seems to mean to remove something, the concept of subtraction is a more abstract idea. Just because students can rattle off subtraction facts in two minutes tells us little about their understanding of what subtraction is.

I recall being asked to develop some lessons for a textbook series in which fourth-grade students at the beginning of the school year would demonstrate their knowledge of *place value*. The textbook publisher wanted some clever ways to show that the students understood place value through the millions. I assumed that most students had only an initial understanding of the concept because of the publisher's narrow and procedural way of addressing the concept.

I developed an activity in which the students used tables to find different ways to cash in on a million-dollar inheritance. I intentionally made it challenging and complex enough to enable teachers to assess what students already knew as well as help them to learn more about the ways to record hundreds of thousands of dollars. As I expected, the publishers were not happy because they felt the activity was too difficult for the students. They wanted some variation of the traditional procedure: merely to recognize the "place" where the single digit means millions and the recall the names of the other six places.

Language

If we are concerned with students' learning, then we must take a long, hard look at what we know from studying how children learn language: reading, writing, speaking, and listening. Language is the quintessential human attribute. Even when Bonzo the chimp appears to have a thirty-five-word vocabulary, he does not think with language nor produce the spoken word. Humans use language for communication of all kinds, especially pertaining to what we know, think, and feel.

The Importance of Activities

I have used the term *activities* deliberately. In my first year of teaching, I abandoned the idea of having a well-orchestrated sequence of skills and concepts, following the well-trodden path that the textbooks promised. I had only about a dozen students in each of my five classes who were present nearly every day. Discounting the habitually truant "ghosts" on the roster whom I never saw, I had another dozen who insisted on taking four-day weekends, being absent virtually every Monday and Friday. Then there were another five to ten in every class who would just disappear for weeks or months at a time. For months I tried every trick in my playbook to increase attendance. I finally gave up and decided to think through how to accomplish my mission differently.

I eventually decided to provide whoever was present that day with a positive experience with meaningful mathematics. There would be a beginning, a middle, and an end where I'd wrap up for them what they had learned. In the middle, they would have to "do the math" and wrestle with appropriately difficult activities. The beginning would have to be my shot at getting them to buy in. I'd set the stage for the activity. I would do some things that would motivate them to pay attention and persevere. Even with fifty-five-minute periods (which is more than most schools have for math), I reasoned that I could ill afford fifteen minutes to go over homework.

For most of the classes I began the period with some prop, some physical materials, to arouse their curiosity. Even when telling them a story that would intrigue them, I'd think about how to use manipulatives of some kind. Some of these activities were problems to be solved, but not the simple problems that were thinly disguised "guess which computation to perform" exercise. My activities required that students use their imagination, suspend their disbelief, and analyze phenomena or situations by using mathematical concepts. I chose some activities because they could demonstrate the power of mathematics to explain and predict what might be going on. Or I chose them because they illustrated the beauty of mathematics and elicited an emotional or aesthetic response. I believe strongly in the two values: practicality and beauty.

Over the years I worked on developing and refining these activities by teaching them in a dozens of different schools, varying in urban/suburban communities. I did not think of these activities as "lessons" or "skill building." They ask students to use the mathematics that they know to wrestle with the problem or situation, and by doing this they will learn the mathematics even more deeply.

Finding Activities

Where do I get these activities? Most are modifications of activities or problems that I have seen elsewhere. Others I create from scratch. I have no hobbies in my life, except an obsessive search for good math activities. I have been to dozens of public and university libraries, combing through their collections of mathematics books. I have spent hundreds of hours viewing videos of exemplary math teachers. I have attended dozens of conferences on mathematics teaching. From books, videos, and conferences I have gotten a wide variety of ways to explain concepts, different examples to use, and fresh contexts to explore.

I had one and only one mentor, and he was not a professional math teacher. He was a graduate student in economics who was teaching in the Academic Potential Program (APP) at Brown University one summer before my senior year in college. His job was to get a hundred middle school boys excited about learning math. We all lived in one of the Brown University dormitories for the summer. The boys had been underachievers in their middle schools, were recommended by their schools, and had attained a score of at least 120 on a standard IQ test. In the mornings they attended three classes—history, English, and math—each taught by someone who was gifted at motivating kids so that they'd go back to their school in the fall, "turned on" to learning.

In my role as counselor in the APP, I was to oversee the sports and other recreational activities of a group of twelve boys. I was helping several kids with their homework on the first night, and I became excited about what they were doing in math class. I asked the teacher if I could attend his class. I ended up going to all three of his classes for the entire summer.

Some of his activities I recognized as modifications of ideas in Martin Gardner's monthly column on recreational mathematics in *Scientific American*. Five years prior to that summer, my parents had given me one of his books, a compilation of columns he had written. I now own fourteen of his books and have photocopied selected chapters from five others. In the Appendix I will list the books among the hundreds in my own library that I have found the most useful in creating activities.

Because of my purposeful collection of activities, a teacher once referred to me as "an encyclopedia of math problems." I replied, "It's my hobby." I am fairly passionate about seeing mathematics everywhere. I have a lot of experience developing curricular activities in a wide variety of *contexts*, which has been as enjoyable as teaching them to students. Planning and exploring the concepts has been my time to "do the math." The walls of my office and my home are covered with newsprint, each sheet a collage of mathematical ideas. My office has a dozen thirty-gallon tubs, filled with manipulatives, some commercially made and others homemade from recyclable materials.

The KWC

When I have thoroughly investigated the concept, I run through a process of presenting a real-life situation to students. Then I will use a metacognitive prompt, called a *KWC*. The KWC is the math cousin of reading's KWL. It stands for:

- K—What do I know for sure?
- W—What am I trying to find out or figure out?
- C—What are the special conditions I need to look out for?

These three questions guide the students in small groups in their investigations of the problem. "Doing the K" means that students should read the problem carefully and then state or write the actual ideas that are literally expressed in the problem or activity. If they draw an inference, that should get recorded under the C. Also when "doing the C," they should include any constraints on the problem. In traditional story problems, what students are supposed to do or to figure out is usually worded as a question at the end of the story; I ask students to carefully restate this idea under the W.

I model doing a KWC with the entire class. We slowly go through the problem sentence by sentence, looking for those ideas that we know for sure (doing the K). I will write on the board what they say, regardless of its accuracy because we will go back over it shortly. Next they note what they are trying find or figure out. Then they restate the W in their own words.

The C is the most difficult for teachers and students, but it is not to be skipped over. It is a crucial piece. Under the C would go any constraint upon the values of variables; any information that would have gone under the K except that we've realized is irrelevant to the problem; and any *inferences* that were not literally stated in the problem. It is all right, even necessary, to draw inferences, but some are faulty, and the students must pay special attention to realize when they are drawing an inference so they can check to make sure it is accurate.

After the whole-class experience with the KWC, I require that the students work in small groups and use the same KWC structure. They ask themselves these same three questions and jot down notes, usually on a graphic organizer. After they have tried the KWC with several problems in small groups, I ask them to do a KWC with their homework to help them develop the habit of using this prompt. You will see examples of KWC in the chapters to come.

Using Activities

In the chapters in this book, I will present exactly what I do when planning activities as well as longer units composed of a host of interconnected activities. To make my ideas clear, I will present the Braid Model of problem solving in which cognition, language, and mathematics are woven together very intentionally so that students can develop significant understanding of mathematical concepts and procedures. It shows you what teacher moves are best at getting students to buy into the activity and how to keep them thinking and doing the mathematics. Then they must *debrief*, reflecting on how they did the activity and what they learned from doing it.

I encourage you when reading the activities described in this book to step back from a literal blow-by-blow description of the action and imagine yourself doing the activity as if you were a student in the class. Read for a holistic appreciation of what the teacher is doing rather than an analytical exercise. Then read it a second time imagining you are helping your students to get their heads into it. How would you modify the activity to make it work for your particular students?

I had the experience of working weekly with many groups of wonderful teachers for two years at a time. One group included a very excited young lady named Mary who was most eager to try new things to help her struggling students. Every other week Mary would come to the group and said, "I did [such-and-such] activity just like you did with us, and it bombed." I calmly asked her to describe exactly how she did the activity. She described a scenario to which every teacher could relate.

I turned to the group and asked them if they had any insight to share with Mary. Others in the group gently volunteered that Mary had skipped over something that we had talked about doing. Later, Mary attended to the issue raised and came back the next week with a success story. Two weeks later she taught an activity that once again bombed. And we all went through her missing part again. This same scenario occurred five times. Each time she had what seemed to her as a good reason for skipping something, such as:

> "We didn't have enough time to do all the stuff you did with us, so I figured I'd save some time."
> "We ran out of time so I thought we could just debrief the next day."
> "I thought they knew [that prior concept] already, so I didn't address it at all."
> "This class was very advanced, and I didn't think they'd need to use manipulatives."
> "You said that the first part of the activity was primarily motivational, and my students are very motivated already."

Each reason was based on an assumption about students' learning that turned out to be incorrect.

A different assumption has occasionally arisen. "I did everything you said to do. I even used your exact words, and the students didn't get it." Upon description of how it was done, teachers realized that this was the first time that these students had been asked to *think*. They balked and waited for the teacher to revert back to showing them the steps of the procedure they should use to get the right answer.

Sometimes a simple shift in how you are doing an activity can make a big difference. I recall watching a video of one of the greats in math teaching as she taught an activity to an entire class. My immediate reaction was, "No! Do this in small groups of three or four kids." It would take more time and she'd have to make bags of manipulatives for each group, but it would be worth it for the dialogue that could be generated in each group that would keep everyone engaged. It would also allow for a good debriefing. I'll describe this activity in Chapter 6.

Before we go much further, I would like to share a simple way of making some important distinctions in my work with teachers. Clarity in my use of some critical concepts will help us all as we wrestle with the ideas in this book.

Content and Process/Curriculum and Instruction

In 2001 in an interview with Diane Sawyer of *Nightline,* Professor William Schmidt commented on U.S. performance in a multinational study of student achievement in math, saying, "There is something terribly wrong here. We must change both what we teach and how we teach it." He was deliberately targeting both the content of the curriculum and the methods of teaching math. In similar fashion, the National Council of Teachers of Mathematics (NCTM) advocated important processes involved in teaching for understanding. The NCTM Standards, first published in 1989, included a second volume, devoted to the teaching of mathematics.

I was delighted that the NCTM Standards (2000) was structured to show five process standards and five content strands/standards. The document not only signaled the importance of these essentially cognitive processes but also devoted a third of the document to explaining how learners must use these cognitive processes to build their understanding of content.

This was a giant step forward for mathematics education because there had been a kind of glass wall separating content and process. Universities and states generally required math "content" courses to be taught by the mathematics departments, where you'd find mathematics professors lecturing students on content. But NCTM was essentially saying that talking at students, telling them what procedures to use, was not the preferred process; such an approach emphasized memorization and little else.

In my work I have not assumed that *curriculum* means content and *teaching methods* (*instruction*) means process. I have seen how they are four somewhat different entities that inform one another. Consider the diagram in Figure I.1.

	Content	Process
Curriculum		
Instruction		

Figure I.1

This simple two-by-two matrix reveals several crucial distinctions. Content and process are different entities, but both ought to be acknowledged as part of the curriculum, as in science, where *inquiry* is both a major process and also a concept that students must understand. Therefore, we can treat problem solving, making connections, reasoning and proving, creating representations, and communicating ideas as processes that must be part of the curriculum as well as concepts to be understood. If students understand how to do these processes and what they are, then they will be more likely to use them to build their knowledge of the content strands (number and computation, algebra, geometry, measurement, data, and probability).

Similarly, instruction by the teacher should involve how to help the children understand both the content and the processes, the concepts as well as the kind of thinking that builds that understanding.

Curriculum

The matrix can be used to analyze a mathematics curricular program, revealing what it emphasizes. I would suggest that a good curricular program would have a balance of all four sections of the matrix. See Figure I.2.

	Content	**Process**
Curriculum	Scope and sequence of concepts, procedures, and facts	Problem solving, reasoning and proving, creating representations, making connections, and communicating ideas
Instruction	Helping students use the processes to understand the curriculum, scaffolding, explanations, and examples	Modeling processes, gradual release of responsibility

Figure I.2

I had a conversation with a colleague from the reading department a few years ago about teaching concepts. I was told, "In reading, we have no concepts; we are pure process." I was surprised and retorted, "What about all these figures of speech, like metaphor, analogy, personification?" Reading does emphasize processes that are inherently cognitive in nature, and they use concepts to more deeply understand what people are reading.

I suppose a case could be argued that math teachers are not interested in processes. Content is king! The only process they advocate is memorizing. However, I see dozens of math teachers every week who are trying to help their students develop processes capable of building understanding. Therefore, we can acknowledge that both mathematics and reading involve both processes and concepts.

The NCTM Standards and the Common Core State Standards for Mathematics

Attention to the way we teach our children mathematics is critical at this time because this is a unique moment in the history of public education in the United States. For the first time, nearly every state has adopted the Common Core State Standards for Mathematics (CCSSM), in essence creating a de facto national mathematics curriculum.

The CCSSM has been promoted as a set of curriculum standards designed to bring coherence to the math curriculum by eliminating the repeated and shallow "coverage" of topics and the wide divergence in content across the states. It addresses fewer critical, core topics in sufficient depth for students to truly understand. The authors' main argument is: "For over a decade, research studies of mathematics education in high-performance countries have pointed to the conclusion that the mathematics curriculum in the United States must become substantially more focused and coherent in order to improve mathematics achievement in this country" (CCSSM 2011, 3). International comparisons for the scope and sequence of standards played a major role in the authors' thinking. This content is specified in sufficient detail to delight the many people in the United States who have wanted a national curriculum. However, this approach to change primarily deals with the curriculum/content cell in Figure I.2.

The CCSSM also includes a set of eight practices that students should manifest in doing mathematics. Proponents of the CCSSM wanted it clearly understood that the document would not advocate teaching techniques, presumably to avoid the "math wars" encountered by the NCTM. These eight mathematical practices are:

1. make sense of problems and persevere in solving them
2. reason abstractly and quantitatively, making sense of quantities and their relationships in problem situations
3. construct viable arguments and critique the reasoning of others
4. create mathematical models by applying the mathematics students know to solve problems arising in everyday life, society, and the workplace
5. use appropriate tools strategically (consider the available tools when solving a mathematical problem)
6. attend to precision
7. look for and make use of structure
8. look for and express regularity in repeated reasoning.

The CCSSM document devoted less than four pages to explain these practices, which are worded as descriptions of highly proficient high school math students. They do not tell us much about how to help students *develop* proficiency in those practices.

Therefore, in no way do they add up to the Process Standards of NCTM (2000) despite the fact that the authors of CCSSM allege that their practices are based on the NCTM process standards and the strands of mathematical proficiency from *Adding It Up* (National Research Council [NRC] 2001). NCTM devoted 135 pages, more than one-third of its 400-page book (NCTM 2000), to explaining the cognitive processes in which students need to meaningfully engage in order to understand and learn the math content (Problem Solving, Connections, Reasoning and Proof, Communication, and Representation). All ten NCTM Standards (content and process) are initially explained in a global fashion and then examined in detail in four grade-level bands (pre-K–2, 3–5, 6–8, and 9–12). These provide a developmental progression of students' learning.

To illustrate the glaring differences between the CCSSM practices and the NCTM processes and NRC proficiencies, consider a brief overview of the latter two. I have organized the processes and proficiencies by the broad process labels used by NCTM. I have combined Problem Solving and Representation because of their overlap.

Connections. Teachers should enable all students to:

- recognize and use connections among mathematical ideas (NCTM)
- understand how mathematical ideas interconnect and build on one another to produce a coherent whole (NCTM)
- recognize and apply mathematics in contexts outside of mathematics (NCTM)
- develop a deep understanding requiring that learners connect pieces of knowledge, so that they can use what they know productively in solving problems (NRC)
- comprehend mathematical concepts, operations, and relations (NRC)
- carry out procedures flexibly, accurately, efficiently, and appropriately (NRC)
- see mathematics as sensible, useful, and worthwhile, coupled with a belief in diligence and one's own efficacy (NRC)
- become motivated to develop a productive disposition (NRC).

Reasoning and Proof. Teachers should enable all students to:

- recognize reasoning and proof as fundamental aspects of mathematics (NCTM)
- make and investigate mathematical conjectures (NCTM)
- develop and evaluate mathematical arguments and proofs (NCTM)
- select and use various types of reasoning and methods of proof (NCTM)
- develop adaptive reasoning (the capacity for logical thought, reflection, explanation, and justification) (NRC).

Problem Solving and Representation. Teachers should enable all students to:

- build mathematical knowledge through problem solving (NCTM)
- solve problems that arise in mathematics or in other contexts (NCTM)
- apply and adapt a variety of appropriate strategies to solve problems (NCTM)
- monitor and reflect on the process of mathematical problem solving (NCTM)
- create and use representations to organize, record, and communicate mathematical ideas (NCTM)
- select, apply, and translate among mathematical representations to solve problems (NCTM)
- use representations to model and interpret physical, social, and mathematical phenomena (NCTM)
- develop strategic competence (the ability to formulate, represent, and solve mathematical problems) (NRC)
- develop adaptive expertise and metacognition (knowledge about one's own thinking and ability to monitor one's own understanding in a problem-solving activity) (NRC).

Communication (NCTM). Teachers should enable all students to:

- organize and consolidate their mathematical thinking through communication (NCTM)
- communicate their mathematical thinking coherently and clearly to peers, teachers, and others (NCTM)
- analyze and evaluate the mathematical thinking and strategies of others (NCTM)
- use the language of mathematics to express mathematical ideas precisely (NCTM).

These processes would constitute the substance of the curriculum/process cell in the matrix in Figure I.2. They must be an essential part of the curriculum for students to develop their ability to do them effectively and thereby to understand the concepts, procedures, and facts of mathematics. A major problem that I see with the CCSSM is the lack of attention to how students could develop their ability to enact these processes.

Instruction

Turning to the Instruction row in the matrix in Figure I.2, we can consider what teaching methods would enable all students to learn the curriculum of both content and process. My personal opinion would be for the curriculum to consist largely of activities that teachers would *coach* the students through, not teach by telling them what procedures to follow. The students should be *doing* the processes that will result in deeper understanding of the content and becoming more adept at doing the processes.

Furthermore, if the curricular program, texts, and ancillary materials do not provide teachers with activities and guides in how to enable students to *do the math*, they will teach the way they were taught, delivering a lecture showing the kids how to use the procedure to get the right answer. It is significantly easier for teachers to address new content than for them to change their teaching methods from "stand and deliver" to "discuss and debrief." Teaching routines are notoriously difficult to change.

About This Book

The purpose of this book is to help elementary school teachers understand the importance of using what we now know about cognitive and language development in order to broaden their repertoire of strategies for teaching mathematics. There have been three different ways that teachers have experienced my ideas about mathematics, teaching, and learning. The first way has been reading about what to do, how to do it, and why. The second way is experiencing the mathematics as students through activities that one would do with children, which include very little "show and tell" and much more "do and debrief." The experiences have been in professional development workshops and courses led by me or by the teacher leaders I have mentored. The third is when teachers lead their own students in doing these same activities that the teachers read about or experienced. If they adapt the activity to fit their students and have them do the appropriate kinds of thinking and discussing when they debrief, students inevitably surprise them with their level of understanding and the quality of their thinking. This third way is where the teachers see the real power of the ideas.

These three ways of experiencing my methods and ideas are not mutually exclusive. Many teachers have formed book studies to discuss the ideas as they try them in their classrooms. In the workshops we encourage the teachers to adapt these methods for their classrooms. In courses, we require that teachers do so.

There are no shortcuts, no quick fixes, if we truly seek for our students to understand. There are obstacles that must be overcome, beliefs and attitudes that must change, and a number of things that need to be unlearned. I cannot offer anyone a five-step program. The dynamics of teaching mathematics effectively are more complex than even a twelve-step program.

This book attempts to tie together what we have learned from those who study cognition and language development with practical strategies for effectively teaching mathematics—content and process—in elementary school classrooms. In the past decade the NRC has produced several major volumes synthesizing research on human cognition and conceptual understanding in content areas of the curriculum: *How People Learn: Brain, Mind, and School* (Bransford et al. 2000); *Adding It Up: Helping Children Learn Mathematics* (NRC 2001); *How Students Learn: History, Mathematics, and Science in the Classroom* (Donovan and Bransford 2005). We shall draw heavily upon this research.

Some of the ideas we discuss may seem a bit abstract. Therefore, we will illustrate them with stories written by a dozen classroom teachers from grades K–6 describing activities that helped students to understand math concepts. Some explain a single point that I think needs to be illustrated. Most need to be read more holistically than analytically because they show how the teachers have made their own interpretations of my ideas.

We will examine several key ideas that cognitive scientists have shared with math educators. We will use these insights about cognitive processes throughout the book because they have great explanatory power to show not only what to do and how to do it, but also *why* it works. Cognitive processes will be the touchstone for all the chapters of this book.

We will also examine a range of language-related practices connected to reading, writing, speaking, and listening, which are all designed to encourage deeper understanding of mathematics. As the students engage in discourse with each other and you, they should move from natural language to more precise mathematical language. Along the way, students must come to see the relationship between the math that they know and the ways they express this knowledge through language, signs, and symbols.

Insights about cognition have driven much of the work in reading comprehension for decades. Significantly more research has been done on *metacognition* in the area of reading than in mathematics. I am not suggesting that we should all just teach mathematics the way we teach reading. However, with some significant adaptations that account for the nature of mathematical concepts, what has been done in reading can be done successfully in math. Teachers have infused dialogue and discourse on mathematical ideas into the students' experiences.

Using cognitive principles and processes along with appropriate language practices can be very powerful, but these are not a bag of tricks that you pull out of your pocket when they are needed. Activities that richly draw on these must be carefully planned, thought through, and tested out. It takes time and perseverance.

We will examine the processes that must be addressed to maximize the potential of all students and help them not only to survive but to thrive in doing mathematics. One or two tweaks to the way we have taught mathematics in the past is not enough. We must pay attention to dozens of facets of the concepts we teach. I will ask you to broaden your sense of what problem solving is. Any mathematics program you use will emphasize problem solving, and an effective teacher must rethink the nature of problem solving and the kinds of thinking he or she wants children to engage in.

We will see how you can help students connect to the context of a math problem. Several different kinds of connections are discussed. Making connections is an NCTM process standard and a key comprehension strategy in reading. From a cognitive orientation, students need to have at least "a threshold of knowledge" about the context in which they are working. In other words, we must ask ourselves what critical aspects of the context must be understood for our students to deeply appreciate the concepts in the problem. Students must be able to make several different kinds of connections to a context and need multiple contexts of a concept in order to build a generalized understanding.

We will invite you to explore the Braid Model for teaching mathematics, especially for problem solving. This approach to teaching math is very flexible and comprehensive. When using this approach, you will think about representing concepts in multiple ways.

These practices and adaptations cannot be done on the fly. It takes a lot of planning, preferably by a group of teachers. We will elaborate on how to develop units and activities while considering the dimensions of cognitively based planning. Teaching the textbook is insufficient. Even the best possible series needs to be supplemented.

We will begin by examining some major findings from the research on human cognition and how they apply to the learning of mathematics. Various aspects of cognitive processes are illustrated in the activities of four elementary school teachers.

CHAPTER

1

Attending to
Cognitive Processes

Memorization of basic facts usually refers to committing the results of unrelated oper-
ations to memory so that thinking through a computation is unnecessary. Isolated
additions and subtractions are practiced one after another as if there were no rela-
tionships among them; the emphasis is on recalling the answers. Teaching facts for
automaticity, in contrast, relies on thinking. Answers to facts must be automatic,
produced in only a few seconds; counting each time to obtain an answer is not accept-
able. But thinking about the relationships among the facts is critical. A child who
thinks of 9 + 6 as 10 + 5 produces the answer of 15 quickly, but thinking rather
than memorization is the focus (although over time these facts are eventually remem-
bered). The issue here is not whether facts should eventually be memorized but how
this memorization is achieved: by drill and practice, or by focusing on relationships.
—Catherine Fosnot and Willem Uittenbogaard (2006)

STUDENTS MUST THINK about the mathematical concepts they are learning in order
to build their understanding. They are adept at memorizing and parroting back
what they've heard or read, but rarely do they understand a new idea from a teacher's explaining it. They must connect the explanation to what they already know
from many previous experiences with related ideas (their prior knowledge).

I remember my fourth-grade teacher introducing us for the first time to percentages. She thought that my friends and I were just brilliant because we followed
along readily with her well-worded lecturette. But this was not our first encounter
with percentages because we obsessively played the board game of Monopoly and

landed dozens of times on the Income Tax square, which required us to calculate 10 percent of our cash to pay the bank. When the teacher told us how percentages worked, I was ready for a formal explanation that not only connected with my prior experience but also cleared up the incorrect information passed on by older children (designed to trick me into giving away my money to the bank).

How did the teacher's explanation fare with the children who had no prior experiences with this concept? Their first encounter resulted in lots of "I don't get it!" noises. These reactions supported her belief that there were "fast" kids who were inherently good at math and the "slow" kids who were not. She didn't realize that she could never make ten-year-olds *conceive* of the concept the way she did. No amount of talking to us, telling us, or showing us how to get the right answer would ever accomplish what Mr. Spock of *Star Trek* fame could do with the Vulcan mind-meld. He could put his conceptions directly into the mind of another or extract their conceptions for him to examine. The students who were quick to "get it" had enough knowledge to validate in her mind her teaching by telling.

The National Research Council (NRC) resources noted in the Introduction cite three major principles that support building conceptual understanding. They are: engaging prior understanding, organizing knowledge into facts subsumed in conceptual frameworks, and using metacognition.

Engaging Prior Understandings

New understandings are constructed on a foundation of existing understandings and experiences (Donovan and Bransford 2005, 4). Students build new knowledge and understanding on what they already know and believe. Pioneering cognitive psychologist David Ausubel once stated, "The most important single factor influencing learning is what the learner already knows" (1978, 27). It sounds obvious now, but it wasn't thirty-five years ago. Ausubel focused on people who were engaged in meaningful verbal learning at a time when most psychologists who "studied learning" ran rats through mazes or had college sophomores try to memorize nonsense syllables for later recall.

Ausubel introduced ideas such as *advanced organizer*, *ideational scaffolding*, and *subsumption* (relating new ideas to one's existing cognitive structures). According to Ausubel, meaningful learning and conceptual understanding occur when the learner consciously and explicitly ties new knowledge to relevant concepts in his or her schemata. Consequently, conceptual learning is somewhat idiosyncratic and requires personal recognition of links among concepts.

We have now come to understand that learners formulate new knowledge by modifying and refining their current concepts and by *adding new concepts* to what they already know. Piaget helped us see that sometimes students can readily *assimilate* new knowledge into their prior knowledge, elaborating on what they already know. For instance, if a student has a reasonably good working knowledge of equivalent fractions, he or she may be able to grasp that $\frac{1}{10}$ and .1 symbolize the same relationship. However, a student with only a minimal understanding of fractions will not be able to do so. A reorganization of the student's cognitive structures may be necessary in order for him or her to *accommodate* the new relationship.

For example, when teaching in Philadelphia, the curriculum called for me to teach my students decimals up through the fourth decimal place, assuming that they "understood" what a decimal place was. None of my students had "mastered" one- or two-place decimals, though they had been "taught" the procedures for several years. Teachers had followed the traditional approach of basing their explanation of decimals on students' knowledge of fractions, beginning with the first decimal place as tenths.

I adopted a different approach. I used a context that my students were well versed in—*money*. They never had enough of it; but they knew the value of a dollar. I started with two-place decimals and related them to a familiar item they liked buy: a candy bar for 25¢ (or $.25). The only constraint I added was that instead of carrying around 25 pennies, they had to have both dimes and pennies. Items that cost $1 or more would be written as $1.25 (for example). The students were all very familiar with this notation. They had seen signs in stores and newspaper ads many times. They knew that "$" meant we were dealing with money and that the "period" separated the dollars from the cents, which we would now refer to as the *decimal point*. We worked on ways of writing dimes and pennies using two-place decimal notation until I was convinced that they all understood the notation as well as the equivalence of 10 pennies and 1 dime, and 10 dimes and 1 dollar. Then we dropped off the dollar sign and did a few more dimes and pennies.

Then we went to the first decimal place and I asked, "What would .7 signify?" Most of the kids had no problem recognizing that this ought to mean that I was thinking about 7 dimes, which was worth 70 cents. We mentioned that one way we write that amount could be $.70. This led to a discussion about including the "tenths" and "hundredths" when we use the dollar sign, even if there are no dimes or pennies. A critical connection was made between including a 0 in a written number to having none of that amount. They had no problem answering, "What would you rather have, $.70 or $.07?" when I asked. So, I knew they were ready for a shift in language. I asked, "Which would be the greater amount .7 or .07?" The explanation

Decimals
w/money

that one means 7 out of the 10 dimes that make up 1 whole dollar and the other means 7 out of the 100 pennies that would make up 1 whole dollar was now meaningfully connected to their experiences. With this beginning, we based our fraction talk on their knowledge of money and one- and two-place decimals, the reverse of the traditional approach.

It is important that teachers determine the nature and extent of their students' prior knowledge in order to plan effectively for the problems, tasks, and questions most likely to activate the best schema for particular students.

> First grade is where we need to build a firm foundation—and where so many students fall apart. Teachers wonder, "Should I just forget about conceptual understanding and give them some concrete procedures to memorize and follow?" Megan Bostrom teaches first graders at Whittier Elementary School, in the Wheaton (Illinois) School District. She has been trained in Math Recovery using the assessments of the Learning Framework in Number (LFIN).

My first-grade student Luke was polite, kind, and conscientious—a dear. He had to work much harder than the rest of the kids in my class to process the spoken word. If you didn't know him or the work he's doing to combat his auditory issues, you might have thought he couldn't pay attention, that he had very low stamina for solving difficult problems, or that his abilities were below average. When a teacher's directions are hard to sift from occasional hallway noise, the hum of the blower, a friend's whisper, or a crumpling snack wrapper, and you've tried your hardest to "just listen!" for years, paying attention gets exhausting. It's not that Luke didn't try; it's that trying hadn't worked for Luke.

Luke had missed some huge foundational numeracy pieces, so on top of not knowing *what* to do during any given math workshop, he didn't have a prayer with the *how* and *why*. He knew that he was behind. And he hated math. No, he *dreaded* math. What added to his anxiety was that I wouldn't drill with stacks of worksheets; teach him procedures, tricks, and shortcuts; or ask him to memorize a set of flashcards, though those tasks would have been so much more comfortable for him than having to think or understand.

Was Luke *at the concrete level* and *not ready for conceptual learning* as some of his well-meaning supporters reported at the table discussion? Should we just have found ways to get him to the correct answer and settle for Luke only memorizing facts and procedures? Would Luke never truly wrestle with real-world problems? Or did I believe what I know about constructivism? That Luke's learning needed his active participation in problem solving and critical thinking in activities that he found relevant and engaging? That he was capable of constructing his own knowledge by testing ideas and approaches based on his prior knowledge and experience, applying these to a new situation, and integrating the new knowledge gained with what he already knows?

The Common Core Standard for Operations and Algebraic Thinking (1.OA.6) specifies that first graders should be able to *add and subtract within 20, demonstrating fluency for addition and subtraction within 10.* It was spring, and by this point in the year we expected students to fluently add within 10. (Subtraction, while taught all year, would be assessed later.) To be truly *fluent* with facts, students need speed, accuracy, and flexibility. They should be able to provide an answer within two seconds when tested orally, or three seconds when taking written tests. To be flexible, students should be able to explain at least two ways they found their answer.

Through an interview with Luke, I found that after weeks of daily support outside my classroom, he was reverting to the least efficient addition strategy: *counting three times.* So if Luke saw 2 + 3, he would use his fingers or grab cubes to count *1, 2.* Then he'd count *1, 2, 3.* Then finally *1, 2, 3, 4, 5.* Not good. This is the *last* kid I need to be heading *backward*! In an attempt to ease anxiety, he'd been shown just how simple addition could be. "See 2 + 3? Just count 2 cubes, now 3 cubes . . . now count them all!" Even at the beginning of the year he had been using the next-level strategy: *counting two times.* I would hear *1, 2 . . . 3, 4, 5.* Now he wouldn't even be close to the next stage: *counting on (3 . . . 4, 5).* While *counting on* isn't enough for fact fluency, it's certainly closer.

Our team decided to use a written test to filter out students we did *not* need to individually interview. We then met with Luke and other children who did not show at least 90 percent accuracy on that test. We printed facts horizontally on 3 × 5-inch cards: one side would read 2 + 4 and the other 2 + 4 = 6. If the child didn't answer within two to five seconds (we didn't want to give kids opportunities to practice cumbersome habits such as using fingers, counting three times, counting two times, or even counting on), we turned the card over to show the entire equation with the solution, helping add a visual memory for each fact. Then at least our assessment could also be a learning opportunity.

After assessing each child, our team reconvened to examine our data. We were, well, horrified. We felt like shutting our door. Closing the windows. About 15 to 20 percent of our kids were not even fluent with addition through 5, never mind 10. Many could not even answer 2 + 3 within two seconds. According to the Common Core, this is a *kindergarten* expectation, and here we were approaching spring of first grade. Do we go with the old, pre-RTI/PLC approach and tell ourselves we did the best we could, but these kids just didn't catch on? Do we just hope the second-grade teachers can help them "when they're more ready to learn it"? (That one used to be my most comfortable statement of denial.)

Or perhaps a scarier goal, do we intervene with the intention of bringing these kids to grade level? We were forced to examine whether we really believed every child could learn.

Did this group of 15 to 20 percent deserve to reach the standard just like their classmates? We knew the answer, although the task was daunting.

Over the next six weeks, we went to battle. We took a deep breath and backed way up. This was hard, because then we had to admit our mistakes: that we had unintentionally let this crew get wedged in for too long. Our team decided we would differentiate in a small group within our own classrooms to best meet the needs of the kids needing intervention; we were worried these guys would be lost in a larger group, and we didn't have time to experiment. My little intervention group comprised Luke and four great girls, each with their own story but with this in common: They did not recognize relationships among numbers. We hoped that was about to change. They deserved to understand number.

I wanted Luke and crew to use number relationships and *thinking* to know their facts. Our math workshop had four portions: we inspected equalities together, then groups rotated through number work, problem solving, and fact fluency. We also spent five to ten minutes in counting routines at the start of the morning. Since the math workshop structure and small-group work were already in place, our cluster of five was fortunate to seamlessly begin its work of understanding the relationship among the facts. We met together three to four times each week for about twenty minutes each time. Their other individual and small groups during our workshop also worked on tasks exactly at their level.

First, we built to 5.

- We used the words *part-part-whole* whenever possible. These kids were still shaky with this foundational concept. We illustrated equations like $3 + 2 = 5$ as

5 whole	
2 part	3 part

  I modeled a few times with two different colors of Unifix cubes, but didn't give them to the kids as I didn't want them counting three times or counting two times to find the answer. If you're sticking cubes together, you sort of have to count each one even if you don't want to.

- Our class examined a string of equalities each day. For about five minutes at the beginning of our workshop, we sat on the carpet and discussed whether the equations I wrote were true or false. Here's a snippet from the beginning of the year.

$$4 + 3 = 7 \text{ \textit{True!}}$$
$$3 + 4 = 7 \text{ \textit{True!}}$$

(How did you know that so fast? Joe, do you want to come show us how you knew that?)

$7 = 3 + 4$ *False!*

(Sarah, I noticed you were the only one who said true. Can you tell us why you think this is true?)

$3 + 4 = 4 + 3$ *False!*

We had to ask the skeptics if they agreed or disagreed that $7 = 7$ and prove our point from there, while still respecting kids' firm convictions. From then on, we didn't use the word *equal*, we said *is the same as*. In the days that followed, we read and discussed equations like $6 = 4 + 2$ (*6 is the same as 4 plus 2*), and more kids begin to understand the true meaning of the equal sign. Especially that it doesn't mean *here comes the answer*.

- We played lots of games with numeral cards. My favorites are from *Ten Frames Number Deck,* by Andrews and Huber (n.d.). We used the cards and games almost every day; the format is so clear, and the authors suggest very doable differentiation for your least and most mathematically experienced children.

Some of our own simple games included grabbing several sets of number cards 0–5, shuffling them, then showing a partner one card at a time to see how fast she or he could name the other part of a predetermined whole. For example, if our decided whole was 5 and I showed you 1, you'd say, "4!" There's also Memory, but faceup. Each partner takes turns finding the missing addend that would add up to 5.

Since we had five kids in our group, I'd have two sets of partners play a game or complete an activity while I assessed the fifth child to see his or her progress.

- We used five-wise Ten Frames only for subitizing—not for counting dots; not for using game chips to "fill the frame" as many websites suggest.

- We used Math Recovery games and activities. Math Recovery tasks are all about seeing relationships between numbers.

- We sent home a different game each week for four weeks. In a plastic bag we placed simple instructions and all needed supplies.

- Kids kept "fact fluency cards" in their desk of their equations through 5. They looked exactly like the cards we used to assess kids whose forte was not the written timed text. One side would read $5 - 2$ and the other $5 - 3$. We'd often connect these equations to our part-part-whole model. "Wow! So if I have the whole, and I take away a part, then I just have the other part? Wait, does that always work? Even for this next equation? No way. Show me."

We had kids spread their cards out on their desks, then pick out the facts they knew well. With the remaining cards, they tried to find patterns between the equations. They might group 2 + 3 and 3 + 2; they might also notice that equations like 5 – 4 and 4 – 3 and 3 – 2 all equal 1.

After kids knew their addition facts to 5 and subtraction facts from 5, we worked on 5+ facts to 10. From here on out, we adjusted the activities above, and:

- We gave the kids their five new fact fluency cards (5 + 1, 5 + 2, 5 + 3, 5 + 4, 5 + 5).

- We added the Ten-Bead Rack to our instruction. While the original Rekenrek has 2 rows of beads, this smaller version has just 1 row: 5 red beads and 5 white beads. For our first activity, I called out a number—6, for example—and asked kids to move that number of beads in just 1 push (we wanted them to subitize, not count). Kids soon learned that a push of 5 white beads and 1 red bead made 6. Students made mental images of numbers, understand combinations of 10, and practice bench-marking 5 and 10.

- Then came addition facts *to* 10 (the sum had to be 10). Kids received their new fact fluency cards and continued with number activities. Then we continued with facts *through* 10 (the sum could be 1 to 10). We followed with facts beyond 10, using the same activities as well as introducing the Twenty-Bead Rack (or Rekenrek) with 2 rods with 5 white and 5 red beads on each rod.

I could see Luke was making progress in our group, but because his anxiety and stamina could fluctuate daily, I needed to get him alone to determine what remained challenging. He bravely accepted my invitation to arrive a half-hour early for school on four different mornings, and we often previewed that day's activity so he could be his group's expert. I was again reminded of how hard he worked, especially the day he almost knocked my socks off. He knew his facts though 5, and was working on 5 + 1, 5 + 2, 5 + 3, 5 + 4, and 5 + 5. 5 + 1 and 5 + 5 were no brainers; but the facts in between were muddier. When I showed him 5 + 4, I was expecting silence, but instead heard a confident "9!"

"Huh? How did you know that so quickly?"

"That's easy. 5 + 5 is 10, so 5 + 4 has to be 9."

I really did try to be calm and cool, but I couldn't help it.

"Luke! Do you even get what you're doing?!"

"No."

"You're using strategies! You're beginning to understand how the numbers fit together!"

I took a risk and started asking him more facts, even through 10. He knew them without hesitation. I asked him his subtraction facts. He knew them without hesitation.

In our intervention group, three of the four girls had similar successes; you have never seen such proud faces. (Mine was one of them.)

My final risk came at the end of our school year, I asked Luke if he still hated math. "Well, I don't *love* it."

I'll take it!

Megan started planning for Luke based on his the LFIN assessments of Math Recovery, which gave her insight into his present understanding and thinking based upon his prior knowledge, not simply his mistakes. Furthermore, the LFIN is a framework that showed her the sequence of strategies he needed to understand how to use. For teachers of young children, ages four to eight, the LFIN is an excellent resource that they should use. (See Wright et al. 2006.)

Organizing Knowledge

Students need to develop a "deep foundation of factual knowledge organized into coherent conceptual frameworks that reflect contexts for application and knowing when to use which information" (Donovan and Bransford 2005, 6). Although knowing facts is important, understanding mathematics is much more than knowing facts and procedures. Success in mathematics requires factual knowledge be understood within a *conceptual framework* of interconnected ideas.

When students' math knowledge is organized, it is readily remembered and appropriately applied. When students learn with understanding, they are more able to apply knowledge to new situations (also referred to as *transfer of learning*) than when they merely memorize things they don't understand. We all have ample examples of students not being able to transfer their "learning" in one situation to a novel situation. We have come to see the need for "bridging activities," where the teachers explicitly help the students develop the connections. We'll illustrate this special kind of teaching and learning in subsequent chapters.

In order to use what they learn, students must achieve an *initial threshold of knowledge*, practice using that knowledge in a variety of contexts, and get feedback on how well they did (formative assessment). Students need to acquire extensive knowledge and know how to organize, represent, and interpret new information. It is essential for learners to develop a sense of *when*, or *the conditions in which*, certain knowledge can be used; this is called *conditionalized knowledge*. To make a point, I sometimes ask students to get into groups of four, add their phone numbers together, and divide that sum by four in order to get the group's average phone number. Some laugh, others dutifully calculate an answer. The procedure may be done correctly, but the answer itself is meaningless. Teaching concepts and ensuring the concepts are understood leads to students finding meaningful answers.

Emily Wiegand is a resource teacher with first and second graders at the Westchester Primary School in Westchester (Illinois) School District. Emily describes how her students built up their understanding of number relationships by creating their own conceptual framework of a neighborhood with streets and houses.

Throughout the school year, my first- and second-grade students had become much more adept with solving addition facts to 20 and were seeing the commutative properties of the facts consistently. However, one area of their understanding that I noticed was not strongly developed, and therefore was not being used in their problem solving, was the relationship between two facts. For instance, if a student was trying to solve 9 + 6, rarely did they first think of 10 + 6 (an anchor fact) and then subtract to find the sum. As many times as I modeled this strategy, I was often met with blank stares and then watched as the student instead counted on. So, I decided to create a fun "visual" activity to see if it would help those students who were ready to better see the relationships between different facts.

I decided to have them create a "math fact" neighborhood. I cut out houses and wrote a student's name and the parts and whole of a particular fact on each house (parts in the bottom corners, the whole in the peak of the roof). I gave students their houses and told them they were going to position them into a neighborhood by figuring out where everyone lived. We rolled out a big piece of colored paper and sat around it in a circle. I said that to move into our neighborhood, they needed to place their house in what they thought was the appropriate mathematical location and tell why they chose this location. (It was important for them to find their own reasons and connections for why their fact related to someone else's fact.)

I didn't want the students just to create the neighborhood the way I pictured it. I knew that it was very important for them to find their own reasons and connections for why their fact related to someone else's fact. So, to begin, I placed my house down near the center of the neighborhood. At first the students were unsure of what to do. I asked some questions and gave prompts to get them thinking. Then, Anne put her house down next to mine and said she thought she should be my neighbor because we both had the same sum.

Next, Ralph put his house with ours because he, too, had the same sum. I asked him how he knew which of our houses his should be next to. We talked as a class about not only the sums but also the addends. After that discussion, our houses were rearranged as follows: 11 + 5, space, space, 8 + 8, 9 + 6. Other students began trying to place their houses, usually by sums, in the neighborhood as well. I gave some direction by using thought-provoking questions, such as, "If your sum is 10, will you be near my house that has a sum of 16?" but then all of a sudden one of the students "saw" some possible patterns and took over. He started to direct the other students to place their houses with same sums going in rows and with increasing/decreasing sums going in columns. As more students saw the patterns evolving they started working with the addends as well (see Figure 1.1).

Figure 1.1

Before we knew it they had created "Sum Streets" and "Addend Avenues." For a short time everyone sat back and talked about who was their neighbor and why, and then one student said, "But I have an addend of 4 also, so could I also live on 4 Addend Avenue?" "But there is no 4 Addend Avenue," said another little girl. So we talked about where that might be, again engaging their number sense of the magnitude of the sums and addends. Following the discussion, we decided to let the student move his house. Suddenly other students saw other places that they could move to, so the neighborhood was rearranged once again. The whole time this was happening I was watching in awe. After the neighborhood had been "finished again," one of the little boys stated that he hadn't been able to move. We looked at what his fact was, $7 + 7 = 14$, and as a class, began to discuss why he hadn't gotten to move. They figured out pretty quickly that it was because his house was a double fact so his addends stayed the same and his sum was the same. Then the other double fact students realized that they hadn't moved either. Another thing that happened after "the move" was that when we started looking at who our new neighbors were, a few people had the same neighbor, but they were now living on a different side of them. This caused an exploration of the addends being +1 and −1 facts (just what I had hoped would happen!). Wow, all of these connections being made just from making a neighborhood with our facts!

When time ran out the students begged me to keep going. In fact, they had now started cutting out more houses to move into the "empty lots" in our fact neighborhood. Since this activity had provided such a rich learning experience for all of the students, I decided to leave it in the room for them to use as a center activity. I also created small neighborhood sheets with blank houses on which the students could record newly built neighborhoods. And, as I had hoped it might, this activity increased many of my students' number sense and their ability to see the relationships between facts and to use those relationships to solve other facts more quickly and efficiently. They drew on their knowledge of the setup of a neighborhood, which helped them to expand their knowledge of the concept of addition.

Emily helped the children to see relationship between math facts by creating their own conceptual framework that organized their understanding. It is important to realize that she merely, but cleverly, provided the *context* for them to do the math.

Concepts and Connections

Even a cursory glance at the research and theories in the areas of reading, mathematics, and thinking would reveal the central role of *connections* in each realm. Connections build conceptual understanding. The more plentiful and the stronger the connections are among related ideas, the deeper and richer the understanding of a concept. Let's examine what concepts are and why they are so important.

Concepts are abstract ideas that organize a lot of smaller bits of information (facts) in a somewhat hierarchical fashion. A set of concepts are subsumed under a *macro-concept* (an even bigger idea). For example, in language arts we encounter concepts such as *hyperbole, synecdoche, metaphor,* or *metonymy* that are examples of a bigger concept, *figures of speech*. Each of these fairly abstract ideas explains particular expressions encountered in literature, poetry, and even everyday speech. (Try going an entire day without using a metaphor. A day without a metaphor is a night without a dream.)

In mathematics, the science of patterns, we have interconnected branches devoted to the study of specific types of patterns, such as shape, dimension, change, uncertainty, and quantity. These are certainly big ideas or macro-concepts under which we can organize a lot of information. Subordinate to quantity, we'd find the concept of multiplication, one that subsumes a great many facts.

Consulting the dictionary for the definition of a particular concept will give the *denotative* meaning of that concept. However, concepts are rich and complex, filled with deeper *connotative* meaning. I get nervous when someone talks about students needing to "know" particular terms or vocabulary words. I don't want kids to memorize a definition. I want their lives enriched by deeply experiencing the *context* that surrounds the concept.

How do third graders conceive of multiplication? Is it something you do to make the amount you have get bigger? If so, that may create a real problem when the student encounters multiplying by fractions or decimals that are less than 1. The product is smaller than the multiplier and multiplicand. The concept of multiplication and its relationship to division continues to grow more complex each year for about six years as the operation is performed with different kinds of numbers, then with variables, matrices, vectors, and so forth. The concept of multiplication can and should grow richer, more elaborate, and more abstract as students experience it in different contexts.

Consider the following statement $\frac{1}{2} \times 8 = 8 \times \frac{1}{2}$. This must be true based on the commutative property of multiplication. I ask kids to show me with manipulatives what each side of the equation is trying to tell us. The kids work on the left side and decide it would look like Figure 1.2.

$\frac{1}{2} \times 8$

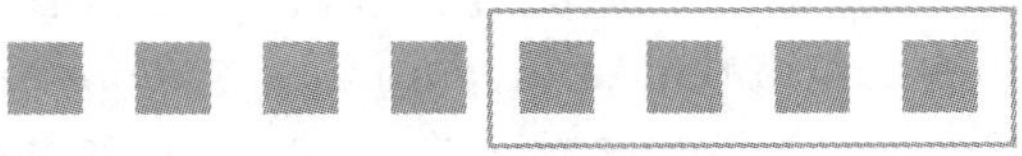

Figure 1.2

The way to talk and think about it is: How big is the group? 8. How many groups do you have? Not even 1; I only have half a group. So we split the 8 whole pieces into 2 halves, 4 and 4. We have $\frac{1}{2}$ of a group of 8.

The other side of the equation might be shown like in Figure 1.3.

$8 \times \frac{1}{2}$

Figure 1.3

How many are in a group? Each group has only $\frac{1}{2}$ of a square. How many groups? 8. So, how many squares? 8 half-squares can make 4 squares. We have 8 groups of $\frac{1}{2}$. To have a group with less than 1 in it may seem odd at first, but it enriches students' conception of multiplication. The area model accomplishes this idea also. The group model also works well with money (e.g., 8 quarters is the same as $2 ($8 \times .25 = 2.00$); 8 groups with $\frac{1}{4}$ dollar in each group have the same value as $2).

Helping students learn the concepts behind the procedures may take some time, but it is definitely worth it. Students who understand both concepts and procedures need less reteaching from you. You and your students will have an easier time with subsequent material because they will have a foundation to stand on.

In the following example, Sara Garner, a mathematics specialist teaching third, fourth, and fifth graders at Whittier Elementary School, in the Wheaton (Illinois) School District, describes an encounter with a pair of puzzled students. Her skillful questioning and scaffolding helps them to see multiplication in a broader manner. Being very familiar with these students' thinking about multiplication and area, she intuits that they are trying to assimilate (add on to existing mental schemata) rather than accommodating (reorganizing mental schemata) and provides appropriate feedback.

I view the process of helping students assimilate new knowledge into prior knowledge as one of the most exciting parts of my job. I was able to build that bridge for students recently as they were working on C.C.5.NF.4 (apply and extend previous understandings of multiplication to multiply a fraction or whole number by a fraction) with a problem involving finding the area of a small plot in a garden. The dimensions for the garden were both fractional parts of a foot. The students had recently learned how to multiply fractions. They had built this knowledge through a series of conceptually grounded activities from the textbook I was piloting. They knew how to find area using a formula, having derived the formula through hands-on experiences finding actual areas. However, as they encountered this particular problem while working in partners, several students had the same response. When they multiplied the two fractions ($\frac{1}{2}$ ft. $\times$ $\frac{3}{4}$ ft.) and got $\frac{3}{8}$ of a square foot, they said, "That's not reasonable. The area can't be smaller than the dimensions were in the first place." Normally, hearing kids say an answer is not reasonable is music to my ears. It means my students are really thinking about what makes sense. In this case, though, it was also an opportunity for me to see that the kids weren't putting together their knowledge of fraction multiplication and area quite yet.

As I sat down with a pair, I asked them to explain their thinking to me. They did so, using the algorithm for fraction multiplication and the formula for area. Then, they told me how they thought their answer was unreasonable because the area of a rectangle should be larger than the dimensions. As I probed further, inquiring as to how they knew this, they gave whole number examples to defend their assertion. So, I asked if we could look at a different problem to see if their claim was always true. Our floor tiles happen to be 1 square foot. I asked the kids to mark $\frac{1}{2}$ foot by $\frac{1}{2}$ foot on a tile. Immediately, they saw that the area was $\frac{1}{4}$ of the whole tile. They now could see that their original answer of $\frac{3}{8}$ of a square foot was reasonable because they were able to blend their more recent knowledge of multiplying fractions with that previous knowledge of area when dealing with whole numbers. They had realized a deeper meaning of multiplication. When we help students build those bridges between previously learned and new concepts, the lightbulbs start to go on and math makes sense.

Note that Sara did not give the students the algorithm to get the correct answer. Instead she allowed them to *see* what they had in their prior knowledge to make sense of the situation.

Using Metacognition

Students develop understanding through appropriate self-monitoring and reflection, often called *metacognition*. Helping students to become effective learners means enabling them to take control of their own learning, to consciously define learning goals, and to monitor their own progress (Donovan and Bransford 2005, 10–11). They actively keep track of their own thinking, adjusting strategies to fit how they are working on a task. Metacognition involves both *self-awareness* of one's capabilities, propensities, strengths, and weakness in a given area and *self-regulation*: the ability to step back and assess one's own work, including monitoring one's own progress.

Efforts by researchers to break down awareness and monitoring into subcomponents have not obtained consistent results. For example, some theorists suggest that knowledge of one's own cognition consists of declarative knowledge (self-awareness as above) but also procedural knowledge (how to implement learning strategies) and conditional knowledge (when and how to use their procedural knowledge). Other theorists suggest that the regulation of cognition might consist of (1) planning: task definition, goal setting, and resource allocation prior to learning; (2) information management: processing information efficiently through organizing, summarizing, and focusing; (3) monitoring: assessing one's own learning or strategy use; (4) debugging: strategies used to correct understanding and performance errors; and (5) evaluation: analysis of performance and strategy effectiveness after a learning experience. As logical as these subcomponents sound, they have received mixed reviews in the research literature.

Many math educators believe that we cannot readily separate metacognition from cognition. They see cognition as including executive control, an ability to monitor and regulate one's cognitive functioning. Regardless of the terminology or partitioning, asking questions can help students to develop metacognitive awareness and to monitor their thinking while working on a task. Better mathematical problem solving happens when students ask themselves questions such as:

- What are the conditions, limitations, and constraints on the problem or situation?
- Is there sufficient information to get an answer?
- Is there one answer, more than one answer, or no answer?
- What are the different ways to represent the situation?
- Does what I am doing make sense?
- What have I done so far? Am I making progress?
- Is my answer reasonable?

Students can be taught how to recognize when they understand and when they need more information. Educators talk about the "gradual release of responsibility," a systematic way of encouraging and helping students to make decisions about their learning, to act upon their decisions, and to be responsible for them. Metacognitive processes are not generic across subject areas and should not be taught as general thinking skills or strategies. They should be modeled by teachers in each subject area.

Connecting These Three Principles

These three principles (building on prior knowledge, organizing knowledge into facts subsumed in conceptual frameworks, and using metacognition) cover a lot of territory—a veritable Louisiana Purchase—and are best seen as interrelated in practice, not treated separately. They inform one another; they facilitate one another as this next story describes.

> Christina Hull is a Mathematics Specialist teaching third, fourth, and fifth graders at Madison School in the Wheaton (Illinois) School District. She incorporates all three principles into her work. She bases her work on some key ideas: not telling students information they could figure out themselves; building upon their prior knowledge; using their understanding of what a formula must do; and helping them to develop deeper conceptions that come from constructing meaning. She also uses the KWC to break down misconceptions.

In the classic movie, *Awakenings*, Robin Williams plays a doctor who helps patients who have been catatonic for years awaken and deal with a new life in a new time. There is a scene in which one such patient, Lucy, will not cross the entire floor to reach her destination, even when it seems as though nothing is stopping her. The doctor has a hunch that it is because the checkered pattern on the floor does not continue past the point where the patient stops. As he colors in the plain tiles to match the pattern that comes before, he explains to a nurse who works beside him why he thinks the patient stops before she reaches her destination.

Dr. Sayer: "There's a void, there's no pattern, there's no visual rhythm, nothing to compel her to keep going."

Nurse: "So we're making something."

Dr. Sayer: "Exactly."

In the next scene, Lucy indeed crosses the floor, passing the previous point of hesitation, and makes it to her destination—which surprisingly was not the place the doctor had thought she was headed.

Patterns in math help our students to awaken and travel the paths to their destination. When there is a void—when they do not see the pattern or recognize the rhythm in what they're doing—there is not a lot to compel them to keep going. Math is the science of patterns. I want my students to experiment with patterns to see when they occur and why they extend. I want my students to see them as a powerful way to understand ideas they have not understood before.

Let's look at a few class sessions on discovering how to find the area of a trapezoid. At this point, my fifth graders know what area is (they've tiled, counted squares, cut figures and rearranged them) and have a solid understanding of the formulas for finding the area of a parallelogram and of a triangle. They know the different types of parallelograms and triangles, as well as the characteristics that land them in different categories. I know they are very familiar with the red pattern block trapezoid, and that (with the shorter base on "top") is the image that comes to their minds when they hear the word *trapezoid*. They are less familiar with a right trapezoid but not familiar with a scalene trapezoid, which has no equal sides or angles.

As we've discussed the parallelogram and triangle area formulas, we've emphasized the question, "Will this formula work with all types of parallelograms? Will it work with all types of triangles?" In order for them to contemplate whether their formula will work for all types of trapezoids, they need to first know what all of those types are.

When I plan, I try to keep in mind this important question: Is there something I am telling my students that they could figure out for themselves? Figuring it out on their own increases the depth of their understanding, which in turn increases their ability to remember the information. So, while I could say to them, "Here are the three kinds of trapezoids," instead it's time to pull out the graph paper and give them a chance to draw.

"We've been discussing the formulas for triangles and parallelograms and have seen that the formulas we've found have worked for all types of triangles and all types of parallelograms. Why does this make sense?"

"Well, they all have the same characteristics. Like all quadrilaterals have 360 degrees."

"So before we try to figure out the formulas for trapezoids, let's make sure that we know what all of the types of trapezoids are. What does it take to make a trapezoid?"

"It has to be a quadrilateral."

"It has one set of parallel sides."

"Exactly one."

"Yeah, it can't be a parallelogram."

I hand out large pieces of grid paper, approximately 2 feet by 3 feet. The large workspace tells the students to draw a lot, try many times; it may not come on the first try.

"OK, draw all of the types of trapezoids that you can that fit that definition."

The students get started right away, motivated by what they know. They draw the right trapezoid and the isosceles trapezoid easily. Then, there is a definite break in the progress.

I find that there is a large range of emotions that students experience when they are being asked to complete a task where they don't automatically know the answer. At a point where their progress is on hold, many will show signs of frustration. Some ask for the answer to be given to them. When I know that they have what they need to figure the problem out, I welcome this frustration. I remind them that they have what they need, but I do not tell them the answer. The frustration would easily dissipate if I said, "I see you've found two types of trapezoids. Let me show you a third." But they have a concept in their minds of a particular type of trapezoid. The frustration not only is in not knowing the answer immediately but also is related to needing to confront a misconception (that all trapezoids look like the ones they have seen), and the breakdown of an idea can be uncomfortable. However, many times, if the previously held idea is not broken down, it won't be removed and replaced.

So, what do I say? I go back our classic questions from the KWC. "What do we know for sure, and are there any special conditions? Use what you know to figure out what you don't know. Draw the parallel lines you know you need. How can you fill in the other two lines you know you need?"

As some students start to find the third way, they talk among themselves. At this point, I don't allow them to look at each other's papers, but they are able to hear the conversations of their classmates. I also want to keep each student engaged, so their next step is to find the area of each of their trapezoids through counting squares. When they do propose a formula, they will need to test it to see if they get the same area.

They are now ready for the target of the day: finding the formula for the area of a trapezoid. They work in partnerships so that they have someone to bounce ideas off. For them to own the formula, they must take a part in discovering it.

As I send them off to begin, I encourage them with the same ideas—math is the science of patterns. We can study what we have seen before. We can observe the conditions that have changed and those that are the same. We can experiment and test. We have seen that we can rely on reasoning that has helped us in the past to think about a new situation.

As I stroll around the room and check in with partners, I am aware that the situation is new and I need to guide them. I need to find the right balance between leading strongly, giving them information, versus letting them to discover it on their own. To keep myself in check, I have preprinted relevant ideas, often in the form of a question. As I plan, I think through the important observations they need to make in order to be successful.

I begin my stops the same way: "Tell me what you're thinking about."

As I approach the first group, I can hear them discussing an idea we had studied earlier in the year.

"Are all quadrilaterals made up of two triangles, or was that just parallelograms?"

"Well, we were just saying that triangles are half of a parallelogram. So maybe that was just parallelograms."

"Let's try it on our pictures. Look, if I divide these trapezoids up, I get two triangles."

"So then maybe it's just length times width like it was before. But I tried that, and it doesn't match what I get if I count the squares."

The conversation comes to a standstill as they feel stuck. I notice that they have brought to light one applicable fact (that trapezoids are made up of two triangles) and have discovered one fact that wasn't as applicable (that the triangles are half of the parallelograms). I want them to focus on the first ideas, so I hand them a card with the question: "What do you notice about the two triangles that your trapezoid is made of?"

I move on.

At my next group, they have tried to calculate the area of each of the figures. They are trying to build from what they know.

"Tell me what you've noticed."

"Well, we've calculated the area using the formula of base times height with each of these parallelograms. We didn't really think that would be it since a trapezoid isn't a parallelogram. But, we thought maybe we could find some sort of pattern."

"Yeah—we were finding the difference between what we got when we counted squares and what we got if we did base times height."

As they describe their findings, I notice that each time, they pointed to the longest trapezoid side as the base.

I find the card that asks, "What is the definition of a *base*? According to that definition, where is the base of your trapezoid?" Before walking away, I stay to make sure that they do remember an accurate definition of *base*. They do, but they are convinced that they have used this definition in what they've been doing. The very fact that I have handed them the card that asks what a base is, however, causes them to give it another look. They are up against another misconception that we have talked about in the past—that the base doesn't have to be on the bottom. They have parroted the definition that a base creates a 90-degree angle with the height, but as they work with the trapezoids, they are stuck to the idea that is should be on the bottom, or perhaps that it is the longest side.

Before continuing on, I make a mental note that there are several things we need to discuss as a class. The attributes of a figure remain the same regardless of how that figure would rotate in space.

I come upon a pair of students who are clearly disagreeing. They tell me: "Robert thinks that it could be finding the area + 2."

"Yeah, I tried that, and it works for all of my trapezoids."

"But I don't think it's that because it doesn't work for mine."

Sally is remembering our earlier discussion and is convinced that a valid formula should work for all trapezoids. I encourage them that this is a critical idea to keep in mind. Then, I focus on Robert's error. He has "crunched the numbers" for his figure and found a connection between them. But, like an in-and-out table with no context, he has not tied his findings to the figures themselves.

"If the formula was base × height + 2, show me on your trapezoids where the + 2 would be."

"It isn't there, I was just looking at the numbers. But why would that work then, if it's not right?"

Patterns bring formality, but they also bring intricacy. Robert needs to look at his figures more intricately. So I ask him to put that question on hold for our whole-class discussion. It is valuable for students to ponder how many times they should test a formula and why they might have a formula that seems to work but isn't correct. I'm certain that the rich discussion with his peers will help Robert more than my quick answer will.

I then ask Sally what she thinks they should look at. She replies, "I've divided all of my trapezoids into two triangles. I really think we need to focus on that. I feel like the formula will have dividing by 4 because the triangle formula has dividing by 2, and there are two triangles here."

I hand them the following key: "Why does the formula for a triangle include multiplying by $\frac{1}{2}$ or dividing by 2?"

One pair has just found a formula, and the entire mood of the room has changed. I knew that putting the discovery into their hands would create frustration. In the beginning, the mood was heavy at times, and I felt as though we were walking through mud. With discovery, there is jubilation. The students are creating a song and dance about their work. The excitement is even more palpable than the frustration. Those who have not yet found the formula are fueled by the fact that they have not been asked to do the impossible after all.

In *Awakenings*, Dr. Sayer handed Lucy a cup of water, believing that she was headed to the drinking fountain but not knowing how to help her to get there. She did cross the floor on her own, but she did not want the water. She wanted to get to the window to look out and see things from another perspective.

Whenever I'm tempted to dissipate my students' frustration by giving them the answer, I remember that I need only help them to find that rhythm that will lead them to see things from a different perspective. That is when the joy of math is real to them. I want to make sure that each partnership has the chance to experience that joy of discovery. So I head to the partnership that has found the formula with another of my cards. This one says, "What relationship do you notice between a parallelogram and a trapezoid?" I want them to work on another way to think about finding the area of a trapezoid. Having tasted the sweetness of discovering a mathematical idea on their own, they meet the challenge of finding another formula head on. No longer are they asking, "Can't you just tell us?" Their attitude is, "Bring it on. Don't tell me, I know we can find it." Eventually, the group has found a variety of formulas, each of which emphasizes how they saw the area of the trapezoid in relation to other figures.

$$(b_1 \cdot h)/2 + (b_2 \cdot h)/2 = A \qquad ((b_1 + b_2) \cdot h)/2 = A \qquad ((h \cdot 2) \cdot (b_1 + b_2)) \div 4 = A$$

As we debrief, the students are able to use their own work to begin looking at ideas about the distributive property and simplifying equations, as well as discussing the different questions that came up during their work with a partner. The conversation is rich as they soak in the beauty of their new view.

They have filled a void. They have studied a pattern. They have found a visual rhythm. Nothing will keep them from going on.

Christina embodies the kind of teaching that incorporates the three principles of learning seamlessly. She broadens students' sense of what patterns are, even using the metaphor of a "visual rhythm" with them. She has prepared prompts to give to individuals or groups to keep them thinking. She appropriately gives them the responsibility for using what they know. She challenges them to think thoroughly, to be aware of what they know, and to use that knowledge effectively.

Each of the teachers has described what she did to help her students develop mathematically. While they focused on cognitive aspects of their teaching and student learning, you may find it interesting to reread their stories noting specific aspects of oral language to communicate mathematical concepts. In the next chapter, we address a variety of language issues.

CHAPTER

2

Attending to Language Issues

[The] human ability—to imagine the future taking several different paths and to make adaptable plans in response to our imaginings—is, in essence, the source of mathematics and language. . . . [T]hinking mathematically is just a specialized form of using our language facility.

—Keith Devlin (2000)

I HAVE OFTEN HEARD that mathematics is a language. For many of us, it is a foreign language that seems impenetrable. Even if both math and language were born of the same evolutionary force, as Devlin suggests, there are obvious differences to which we must attend when teaching children. For example, there are a large number of concept labels that have multiple meanings. Concept labels, such as *plot*, *column*, or *base*, are technical terms in mathematics that can be readily understood by children if we take the time for a word web that helps them distinguish the various meanings (even at the denotative level) before our direct work with conceptual understanding with the mathematics.

Building the Language of Mathematics

The language of math requires symbolic notation to deal with increasingly abstract concepts and patterns. Even with young children, symbols and signs are so much a part of what doing mathematics is that I urge teachers to make certain that *every sign and symbol that they use has a concrete referent in the students' experiences.* Looking at the descriptions that brilliant mathematicians used to communicate their ideas even 200 years ago illustrates how cumbersome explaining math can be.

Conversely, when using symbolic notation with a shared meaning, concepts can be presented precisely, expeditiously, and simply. For instance, try to explain the distributive property of multiplication over addition.

When a person must multiply two natural numbers together to find their product, he can partition one of the numbers in any manner that results in the two numbers that sum to the number being partitioned. Then he can multiply the number that was not partitioned by each of the two separate parts. Finally by adding these two parts together, their sum will be the answer to the original question, "What is the product of two natural numbers?"

If you know the code, then the symbols:

$$a \cdot b = c$$
$$b = x + y$$
$$a(x + y) = c$$
$$ax + ay = c$$

make sense. However, we should not mistake our goal for the process of getting there. We have created a mathematics curriculum that drills children in memorizing a group of symbols they do not actually understand.

The process of getting to the goal of understanding the symbolic language of mathematicians is a complicated one. It does not start with "premature symbolization." It should start with their own natural language and gradually move to more proper mathematical vocabulary, and then to using some symbols that can convey the precision of mathematics.

We have a special obligation with the expansion of technology to make explicit when there are multiple symbols for the same concept or process. For example, division is often seen with a slash (/) after students have been taught that ÷ is the division sign. Similarly, multiplication may be represented by · after spending time with × in their times table. And multiplication may be implied by 3 ×. (And it drives me crazy when a kid tells me, "I *times* it by 3.")

Understanding the Operations

For the operations to be meaningful, students need to talk about the objects they are manipulating. And they must discuss the variations that adults take for granted. Let's look at some of the things we must attend to in our attempt to help students build up the meaning of the operations with whole numbers and fractions.

Addition

The plus sign (+) representing addition is not ambiguous. It represents the action of combining two quantities (two or more addends) into a single *sum*. It is an operation that operates on the two quantities. However, the field is made muddy by well-intentioned parents drilling their children with flash cards to which they say, "1 plus 1 makes 2" (1 + 1 = 2). Not only is this an example of premature symbolization but parents and primary-grade teachers use language that undermines understanding: the card says 3 + 4 = 7 and the adults say "3 plus 4 *makes* 7." The emphasis of the operation moves away from the true operator and is granted to the equal sign. By the time teachers get around to saying "equals" instead of "makes," the damage has been done. Many students have developed a clearly erroneous notion that when presented with "7 = 3 + 4," they will tell you that you can't do that. Worse yet, when asked if "3 + 4 = 4 + 3" is true or false, many will say it is false, thus negating an example of the commutative principle of addition.

This misconception of the equal sign is a costly one. Teachers in the intermediate grades tend to assume that the meaning of the equal sign was thoroughly dealt with in the primary grades but are frequently surprised when they give a diagnostic test of equivalence and the meaning of the equal sign. Consider 3 + 8 = ? + 7. If students have had sufficient experience with composing and decomposing number and number relationships as well as understanding of the equivalence meant by the equal sign, they can see the ? stands for 4. If not, they tend to say that ? means 11. And some will continue adding left to right and say the final answer is 18. This is not a numerical mistake. It is a conceptual one.

Subtraction

Subtraction is more complicated than addition. The minus sign (–) is used to signify the operation, as well as indicating negative numbers. There are several very different situations in which we might do subtraction (or ways to represent the action required when writing an equation). Some math folks suggest that we can refer to these situations as different "models" of subtraction: "take away," "difference," and "part-part-whole." I want teachers to help their students use their language ability to discern how these situations are similar and different. Unifix cubes are great for color-coding the different parts (and for sticking parts together to create a whole amount).

Don't say makes for "="! (handwritten margin note)

The language of subtraction must be directly modeled by the teacher, especially when comparison and difference are not explicitly stated. Consider this situation:

> Katie has 10 jelly beans and Don has 6.
> How many more jelly beans does Katie have than Don?

There are actually five other similar situations about which we could question the kids.

> Katie has 10 jelly beans and Don has 6.
> How many fewer jelly beans does Don have than Katie?

> Don has 6 jelly beans. Katie has 4 more than Don does.
> How many jelly beans does Katie have?

> Don has 6 jelly beans. He has 4 fewer than Katie does.
> How many jelly beans does Katie have?

> Katie has 10 jelly beans. She has 4 more than Don does.
> How many jelly beans does Don have?

> Katie has 10 jelly beans. Don has 4 fewer than Katie does.
> How many jelly beans does Don have?

These situations could be represented concretely by giving the students two different colors of Unifix cubes. For the first situation, you might have the kids create a stack of 10 cubes of the same color to represent what Katie has and a stack of 6 cubes of another color to represent what Don has, and then put the 2 stacks side by side.

Ask the class to respond to the following questions:

How many does Katie have? (10)	How many does Don have? (6)
Do they have the same amount? (No)	Do they have different amounts (Yes)
Are they equal? (No)	Are they unequal? (Yes)
Who has the smaller amount? (Don)	Who has the greater amount? (Kathy)
Who has fewer? (Don)	Who has more? (Katie)
How many more does Katie have?	

At this point the students should push their stacks next to each other and break off the top 4 cubes from Katie's stack so that the 2 stacks are the same height. The amount they have broken off we can now call the "difference," and it represents how many more Katie has than Don. After having the students use this kind of questioning involving different people, objects to be represented by Unifix cubes, and amounts of objects, they may begin the process of symbolically representing the situations (e.g., $10 - 6 = 4$).

The last four situations present a slight change in the questioning. In each situation the students are given one of the two amounts, which can be easily represented with one of the cube colors. The second person's amount is to be found. They know what the difference is (4 in the example given). The students need to think about the relationship they are representing in each of the four situations. For students familiar with the KWC, it usually takes only a few minutes of talking in small groups to realize that 4 cubes may be showing how many cubes can be taken from Katie's stack of 10 to get Don's amount (in the last two situations), or how many cubes must be added to Don's 6 cubes to determine Katie's amount (in the middle two situations).

Multiplication

Teachers can make explicit the language of the different models of multiplication. Creating different representations as they go, teachers should help students see and talk about the equal groups model, the rectangular array model, and the rectangle area model. There is also a fourth model that some programs include: the Cartesian product model.

The first model involves children working with manipulatives, creating groups that have the same amount in each group while using the corresponding language (e.g., 4 groups with 6 in each group; or 4 groups of 6). This situation is written symbolically 4×6. Notice that the "turn around fact" (6×4), is a different situation—it symbolizes 6 groups of 4. Of course, they have the same product (or the same number of objects) because the multiplication of two numbers is commutative. It is very troubling to see some teachers going through these language distinctions at light speed in order to get to the memorization drills in which the kids are told that 4×6 and 6×4 are the same thing. They are not! When the students encounter division, this distinction between 4 groups of 6 and 6 groups of 4 becomes clear if they are moving around manipulatives and talking about them,.

The rectangular array is important because of its orderly approach to helping kids "see" the patterns in multiplication. The array has rows with the same number of objects in each row and columns with the same number in each column. Furthermore, the number of objects in each row is the same as the number of columns, and the number of objects in each column is the same as the number of rows. What a magnificent pattern! Some students come to understand the meaning of multiplication from this pattern of rows and columns. I believe this understanding comes from being able to see the entire pattern organized, rather than the clumps of the group model.

The transition to the rectangle area model can go smoothly when teachers have the kids compose rectangles from square tiles. For example, what are all the rectangles you can make from 24 square tiles? Make a solid rectangle with no holes. Such activities (using one-inch square tiles) help students build upon the rows and column language from the array model while introducing the term *dimensions* by which they'd measure the size of the rectangle (e.g., 6 inches for two of the sides opposite each other and 4 inches for the other). They can then be introduced to the symbolic way of representing the rectangle as 6″ × 4″ (of course making special notice of the symbol for inches). The 6 × 4 rectangle made of squares, like any 6 × 4 array of objects, has 6 horizontal rows and 4 vertical columns, which can be seen by the students who are using square tiles.

Note the similarities and differences among three models as shown in most texts (Figures 2.1, 2.2, 2.3, and 2.4).

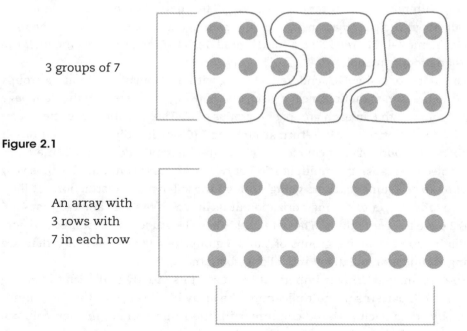

3 groups of 7

Figure 2.1

An array with
3 rows with
7 in each row

or 7 columns with 3 in each column

Figure 2.2

A 3-by-7 rectangle
(with 3 rows
and 7 columns of
square tiles)

Figure 2.3

A 3″-by-7″ rectangle
with area
of 21 square inches

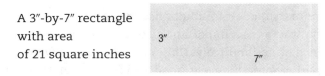

3″

7″

Figure 2.4

One serious problem many teachers have realized is that the traditional approach to teaching multiplication depends on student's understanding of the group model. Most curricula go immediately from the group model to the memorizing of math facts. Teachers tend to assume that students' introduction to multiplication (with the group model) is sufficient. The array model is barely touched upon. And the rectangle area model may not appear in the traditional curriculum until a geometry unit. Even then, area is explained as merely taking the dimensions (e.g., 3″ by 7″ in Figure 2.4) and using one's knowledge of the math facts, multiplying the two sides together and saying "square inches." Figure 2.3 is essential to children's understanding of what multiplication is and why Figure 2.4 works.

The Cartesian product model of multiplication, as seen in a few K–6 textbooks, is usually presented simply, such as making outfits of different shirts and pants and finding the total (or product) using a tree diagram. However, I have had more success with relating these to the array model, using the choices as the row by column arrangement. See Figure 2.5.

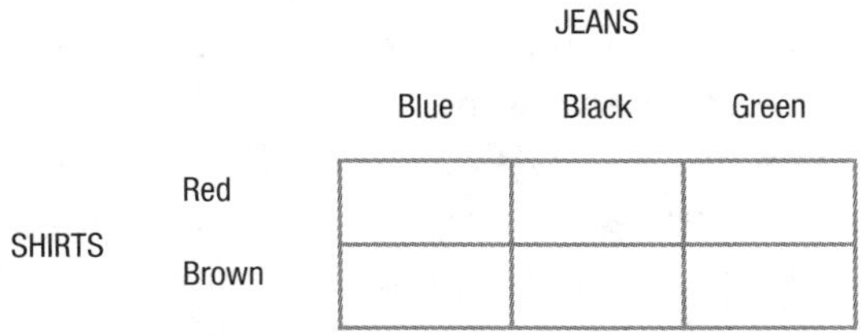

JEANS

Blue   Black   Green

                    Red   ┌────────┬────────┬────────┐
                            │   │   │   │
    SHIRTS   ├────────┼────────┼────────┤
                    Brown   │   │   │   │
                            └────────┴────────┴────────┘

Figure 2.5

Every time we encounter a new kind of number (i.e., fractions, decimal, rational numbers, irrational numbers), we should help students to compare and contrast the representations to whole-number work, especially in multiplication. We definitely want our students to have great flexibility in their representations, to conceive of the connections among kinds of numbers, and to be able to describe situations in which they are using multiplication thoughtfully.

Division

The same three primary models for multiplication can be used with modeling division situations, but there is an important distinction to be understood. The group model shows this distinction nicely. Children first generally encounter division when they are sharing something (e.g., food, candy, money). In this situation, they know how many people are sharing the commodity and how many objects are to be shared. They quite naturally see this kind of division as everyone gets a "fair share." 24 apples divided among 4 children equally will be accomplished by children who have not yet memorized facts by simply giving out the apples one at a time and checking to ensure that it is done fairly. I have heard children refer to this as "divvying them up."

Fair share division is so intuitively grasped by children that many math programs emphasize this version of division (formally called *partitive*) as the main way for students to understand what division is. However, there is another situation that students must recognize as division. Imagine those same 24 apples and we want to give each child 3 apples to take home. How many kids could we give 3 apples to? They can work out the answer by repeatedly giving 3 apples to different kids until they run out of apples. Taking the same amount is not the same as fair share division because in the first situation the kids are trying to figure out what the fair share ought to be. In the second situation they are giving away that fair share amount while trying to figure out how many times this could be done. With kids I refer to the second situation as "chunking" (it is formally called *quotative*). Taking out the same amount each time is sometimes described as repeated subtraction.

When introducing students to division (usually in third grade), how the teacher describes these situations, as with the other operations, critically influences how they think about the operation—what they think it *is*. If the teacher only talks about division as, "How many times does 3 go into 24?" the kids think and say, "3 guzinta 24 8 times!" Good heaven! *Guzinta* is not a technical term; it's not even a word. Perhaps there are a handful of children who gain some conceptual understanding from this kind of oral practice, but it leaves most children woefully confused.

Therefore, I encourage you to spend time planning the language, metaphors, and terms that you use, especially when introducing a new concept. Which of the many manipulatives or materials could you use to demonstrate key attributes of the concept, and how could you describe these ideas? For every different representation teachers should select the best ways of talking about each different feature of the representation so that it connects both with what the students know already and where they will be going with the concept latter in the curriculum.

Fractions

There are three primary models of fractions: part of a shape or whole, part of a set or quantity, and part of a distance or length. Help your students explore these models of fractions with manipulative materials and give plenty of time to talk about them.

Fractions as Parts of Wholes

When using a model showing a fraction as part of a shape, encourage the kids to refer to the part of the whole shape as: "I have 1 of the 3 equal parts it would take to make one whole shape." Stress that students should be able to show classmates two things with the shape model: the size of the part and its relationship to the whole shape itself.

I love pattern blocks for exploring fractions with kids. The concept of $\frac{1}{3}$ is dynamic because the whole can change. The green equilateral triangle can be $\frac{1}{3}$ of the red trapezoid and the blue rhombus can also be $\frac{1}{3}$ of the yellow hexagon. The part is always expressed in relation to the whole shape.

Students need a lot of talk about these relative sizes *before* working with symbolic notation. I strongly suggest to teachers that students record the way they have been talking: "One-third" should be written out. The kids should be able to see that there are two pieces of information separated by a hyphen. The term *one-third* means 1 part out of the 3 equal parts it would take to make the whole shape. The hyphen comes back into play when they are ready to write the symbolic version, in which case it might be with either the hyphen tilted (e.g., ⅓) or horizontal $\frac{1}{3}$; they have the same meaning).

Pattern blocks are also superb for exploring equivalent fractions. Take out the orange square and the tan rhombus. The four shapes remaining are marvelously commensurate with one another: the yellow hexagon can easily be the whole, made with 2 red trapezoids ($\frac{1}{2}$), 3 blue rhombi ($\frac{1}{3}$), or 6 green equilateral triangles ($\frac{1}{6}$). Students are readily able to talk about the relationships because they have been composing and decomposing these shapes for years (e.g., "3 greens make a red" or "A blue and a green make a red"). Students can justify their conjectures (e.g., "A red, a blue, and a green can make a yellow because you can trade the blue for 2 greens and the red for 3 greens and you'd have 6 greens, which we know can make a yellow").

Fractions as Parts of Sets

The second model of fractions is when you have part of a set or quantity. Students need to have a lot of objects with which they can model the total number of objects in the set and the number of objects that are in the various parts. For example, I purchased a large quantity of flattened glass marbles (commonly used in aquaria); they are flat on one side so they don't roll. Students must count how many they have as a *total* (the term we will use in this model instead of the *whole*).

All the groups have received 12 of these marbles: 6 red, 4 white, and 2 blue. (In the initial work with the students, I do intentionally give each group of three students the same quantities. Later I will give them random numbers of each.) On a recording sheet they enter these numbers two ways: as individual numbers and as fractional parts of the total. This model of fractions is sufficiently different from the previous model that some students are surprised when they see the fractional parts add up to the total: $\frac{6}{12} + \frac{4}{12} + \frac{2}{12} = \frac{12}{12}$. Most students who have a strong background with fractions as parts of shapes and good number sense can reason that $\frac{6}{12}$ is the same as $\frac{1}{2}$ because the 12 can be partitioned into 2 equal parts of 6—the 6 red and the other 6 that are blue and white.

Fractions as Parts of a Distance or Length

The third way we use fractions is remarkably different from the other two and requires some good activities that use the language of measurement—fractions that are parts of a distance or length. This model also shows us how fractions are numbers too. We can envision partitioning the unit of measure into a fractional part of that unit. For example, we can see the little lines on the ruler that mean $\frac{1}{2}$ of the inch, $\frac{1}{4}$ of an inch, $\frac{1}{8}$ of the inch, and perhaps $\frac{1}{16}$ of the inch.

We can also relate this model to fractions on a number line. Imagine a number line from 0 to 4. We could put in points for 0, 1, 2, 3, and 4. Next we'd put in points signifying $\frac{1}{2}$ and $\frac{1}{4}$, both less than 1 unit away from 0. These are numbers. Next put in a point "halfway" between 1 and 2. That point would be another number, $1\frac{1}{2}$.

There is one other important meaning for fractions: division. One whole pizza divided among 4 people means that each would get $\frac{1}{4}$ of the pizza. Furthermore, 1

÷ 4 = .25, and if the pizza cost $10 and they shared the cost equally, each person would owe .25 × $10 or $2.50.

Listening to Students

The language that students use is a form of representation of how they conceive of what they see or do. Listen to students as they talk to one another in their small groups to know what relevant prior knowledge they have and how they talk about it. What terms do they use? How they talk about a concept indicates how they are thinking about it.

Identify the critical issues of understanding and misunderstanding. Are there prevailing misconceptions or typical mistakes students make? Prepare a list of words, phrases, and metaphors to use in explaining the critical issues that you have identified. Have ready at hand good questions to ask that will *scaffold* the task or activity or challenge their thinking. Explain only the minimal things that they need to know before they do an activity, and be ready to explain key issues in several different ways during the debriefing after they do that activity.

Discourse in the Classroom

Australian educators Jennie Bickford-Brand (1990) and Sue Gawned (1990) have studied how specific language (e.g., concept labels, terms) is used in the discourse between teachers and students. The language modeled by teachers for their students to use during problem solving included five different modes, each with a different purpose. Teachers need to clearly label what mode they are modeling and the purpose it is serving. With more experience with various modes, students begin to realize the nuances of the terms within each mode.

I have listed the definition in the form of a verb to give a flavor of the denotative meanings. The connotations may be massaged for specific mathematical activities.

descriptive language—a variation of K in the KWC
> *describe*: to convey an idea about attributes, components, features through words
> *notice*: to perceive with the mind
> *select*: to make a choice among several alternatives
> *classify*: to organize according to category

procedural language—following rules, procedures, conventions
> *plan*: to formulate a scheme or program for accomplishing something
> *sequence*: to arrange items in a continuous series

order: to put in a methodical or systematic arrangement

organize: to arrange in a coherent form

explanatory language—to make comprehensible (in words)

clarify: to make clear or easier to understand

summarize: to present the substance in a condensed or concise manner

synthesize: to combine to form a new complex product

justify: to demonstrate or prove to be right or valid

reflective language—to think, contemplate, meditate upon thoughts, ideas, and concepts

wonder: to be filled with curiosity or doubt

imagine: to form a mental picture or image

speculate: to engage in a course of reasoning based on inconclusive evidence

conjecture: to infer from incomplete evidence

reasoning—inferences are often noted in the C of KWC

infer: to reason from premises, circumstances, or evidence

predict: to make known in advance, from special knowledge, data, evidence

interpret: explain the meaning, or conceive of the significance

conclude: to reach a decision by reasoning from evidence

assume: to take for granted or accept as true without proof or evidence

The distinctions among the five modes and the terms noted within each may help you plan for the kinds of thinking and talking that you want the students to do.

Deanna Bero teaches second grade at Lincoln Elementary School, in the Wheaton (Illinois) School District. She has also taught kindergarten and first grade. She is very comfortable helping students talk about math concepts as well as allowing them to figure out on their own the many ways to use measurement tools. This activity shows how she helped build a community of productive discourse in her classroom.

When students are given the opportunity to talk about their thinking in math as they do in reading, they prove time and time again that they can make connections, generalizations, applications, and inferences. Allow them to build deep conceptual knowledge, and they develop valuable mathematical practices and use them to benefit themselves and other students. When children lead one another along the way to solving a problem, they are more willing to take risks, catch mistakes, and make sense of the mathematical concepts.

At the beginning of the year, we created a chart to teach and remind students what a conversation about math should look and sound like:

Sit in one spot.

Keep my hands to myself.

Think the whole time.

Explain my thinking.

Share my strategies.

Raise my hand to share.

Ask questions.

We also created a list of thinking stems to help students talk with one another. We need to teach students explicitly how to have a conversation about math. The stems included:

I am thinking . . .

I am noticing . . .

I am wondering . . .

I can't believe . . .

What are the chances . . .

This is confusing because . . .

This reminds me . . .

This works because . . .

This doesn't work because . . .

A project near the end of the school year—*measuring the room*—sparked a great deal of mathematical conversation in our classroom. We began by discussing the terms *length*, *height*, and *width*, using our classroom door as a model. Students gave examples, drawing illustrations on the SMART Board. Bobby stated, "*Long* and *length* are the same." This sparked the observation that sometimes people use these terms interchangeably, depending on the shape they are measuring and its position. Beginning the lesson by building vocabulary allowed students to practice using the terms in their conversations. They cannot engage in meaningful conversations without understanding the math language.

Then we divided the students into groups of three and assigned the task of measuring the height, length, and width of the classroom, using any of a variety of measurement tools we made available. I watched as each group choose their measurement tools, many of them trying to figure out how they would measure the height of the room. A very strong math student grabbed some measuring cups; when I asked why, she shrugged her shoulders. (She never used the measuring cups, opting for the linear measurement tools her teammates had selected. I saw the importance of allowing children to learn from one another by working in groups.) Some students probably chose something silly and unfathomable to have fun with while measuring, but having fun is important in a math lesson for seven- and eight-year-olds.

Susie decided to measure the room using pencils, a completely reasonable nonstandard form of measurement. I asked her how the pencils could help her figure out a standard measurement unit. She spotted the yarn and said, "I can use the yarn to see how long the pencils are." When she finished rolling out the yarn, she grabbed the bin of 12-inch rulers and lined them up alongside the yarn. She then added all the rulers and found the length of the room in feet. She was proud of figuring out the problem herself.

Bobby measured the tiles in the floor, which were 1 foot square. He then counted the tiles and figured out the length and width of the room in feet. His partner Timmy was amazed that they figured out an easy and quick shortcut to complete such a large and seemingly challenging task. He went around telling the other groups about their ingenious discovery.

We met back as a class to confer and share methods and strategies for measuring the room. We compared how Susie and Bobby found the length and width in feet by using different strategies and tools. One group estimated how many rulers tall the room was. Another group estimated the height of the room using yard and metersticks. We discussed which measurement tools would be more effective than others to measure length, width, and height. We observed that different tools are used for finding different kinds of measurement: a clock measures time, a thermometer measures temperature, a scale measures weight, a cup measures liquid. Sharing their thinking in class allowed students to address misconceptions and increase their knowledge.

Bobby and Timmy shared their big discovery, and I asked the students how measuring and counting floor tiles could help us find the height of the room as well. Bobby said, "Oh, you could measure how tall a brick is with a ruler and then count how many bricks from the floor to the ceiling." It was a golden moment. Children saw that they could solve a seemingly daunting task when they talked about it with their classmates.

Stimulating Dialogue, Discussion, and Discourse

The highest-performing countries in international comparisons of mathematics achievements all feature a culture of teaching and learning designed to help students make connections and build conceptual understanding. This observation is based on the videotaped lessons of hundreds of eighth-grade teachers collected in the Third International Math and Science Study (Hiebert et al. 2003). The researchers found that teachers in top-performing countries not only assigned their students challenging math problems but also used active questioning and dialogue to help students see and understand connections among math concepts as they solved these problems.

In stark contrast, none of the one hundred U.S. eighth-grade math teachers in the videotapes used questions or conceptual dialogue that helped students explore the math concepts. Instead, teachers turned all the problems into procedural exercises—giving students a formula into which they'd plug in the numbers. Another analysis of the videotapes from U.S. classrooms found that a third of the time, teachers simply gave students the answers (Stigler and Hiebert 2004).

I do not seek to chastise eighth-grade teachers but rather to ask, what are the distinctive characteristics of teaching math in U.S. schools? Helping students follow the steps to get the right answer? Taking the pencil out of a student's hand to show him how to do the steps? These cultural aspects of teaching math did not originate in eighth grade but many years earlier. My point is that if we want students to discuss math concepts, they should start doing so in primary grades and continue throughout their schooling. We must begin building math talk into the culture of all our schools.

Amy Tepavchevich teaches second grade at Prairie Elementary School, in the Naperville (Illinois) School District. She candidly writes about her "stretch" to help her young students develop the communication skills that her fifth graders had practiced easily in prior years. She explains the steps she and her students took as she guided them from think-pair-share to sophisticated math conversations as a class.

Having come from an intermediate grade to a primary grade, I was skeptical about how math talks would look or work in my classroom. We spent our days practicing sitting in our seats and not asking what time recess was; how was I going to hand over control and let the students guide their math discussions? I accepted that our math talks in second grade would look different from some of the examples I knew, but I was sure students could participate in meaningful discussion. It was just a question of how to get started.

I started simply. We were reviewing how to make 10, a concept my students had worked on in first grade. I began with partner discussions, being very careful to pair students wisely to ensure productive conversations. I posed a math problem on the board, $7 + 6 =$ _____ and asked students to turn to their partners and brainstorm how they might go about solving this problem.

After a few minutes, we reconvened as a class. "OK, what were some strategies you used?" I was bombarded with hands. "I counted on," "I did $6 + 6 = 12$ and added 1." But this was still the traditional classroom response: Raise your hand and wait to be called on. I decided to build on the think-pair-share idea. I placed a new problem on the board and asked students to turn to their partner and talk about it, but I stopped them before they began. "What does a conversation sound like? How many people are talking at one time?" We talked about respecting the person one is talking to, not talking over each other, making eye contact, and asking questions to gain more understanding. Then I let them think through the problem with their partner. They each had a piece of blank paper, and I asked them to show the thinking they had done as they worked to find a solution. Noise escalated as partners decided on a reasonable method, created an explanation on their paper, and verified that each partner knew how they were solving the problem.

This seemed a solid foundation for a math talk. I reconvened the class, partners sitting next to each other, and asked for volunteers to share their thinking. As students explained the math problem on the board, I asked questions for clarification: "How did you decide on that strategy?" "Why did you do that?" "Can you explain that again? I'm confused." My questions got them talking about their thinking, prompting them to find different ways to explain their answers. As students continued sharing their strategies, I whispered questions in other students' ears, which the students then asked aloud.

This went on for a few weeks—the students solved a math problem in small groups or with a partner, the class reconvened and students shared their thinking on the board, I walked around and whispered questions in students' ears. The day students began to raise their hand on their own was a great day! Now all I had to do was label this question-and-answer discussion. I said the words *math talk*. "It's similar to what we have been doing," I explained, "but with more talking." This got the class' attention. I was encouraging them to talk without having to raise their hand.

We brainstormed possible questions to ask. What strategies are you using? How did you know that? Where did that answer come from? Why did you choose that method/strategy? Can you describe how you solved this problem another way? How did you check your work to make sure your answer was correct? The students recalled all the questions I had whispered in their ears over the past few weeks and formed a few new ones on their own. I typed up all the questions and gave each student a copy.

Again, we started small. They still solved a problem with a partner but then shared their thinking in a group of four or six students. Each student had a dry-erase board showing their math work and the list of questions to guide their discussions. Students shared their answers with the other members of their small group, who asked questions to clarify their understanding. I listened in, periodically posing a question of my own, occasionally asking whether another student could explain what the first student had just said in another way. During a discussion about double-digit addition strategies, one student asked me, "Can we do it that way? Because I get it like that." I thought, *Great! Math talks can work in my primary setting*. But I just said yes.

After a few weeks of practicing math talks in small groups, we began having them as a whole class. When you walk into my room during a math lesson today, the students are talking (without raising their hand), questioning one another, looking to their peers for help, and learning not just from me but from one another. My students love math because they are encouraged to talk to one another—a lot.

Julie Kanturek teaches second grade at Black Hawk Elementary School, in the Marquardt School District in Glendale Heights (Illinois). As a culminating task at the end of the year, she had her students complete a complex task (an adaptation of the "freight train" problem, on pages 20–29 of my book, *Comprehending Math*) that requires a lot of dialogue to make it meaningful.

I told the students they would be solving a really cool problem about freight trains, and I needed to be sure they knew enough about freight trains to do the problem. "What do you know about freight trains?" Responses included: "They are really long." "They carry lots of stuff." A student who was not very good at estimating elapsed time offered: "They take about thirty minutes to pass by!"

I projected the problem, which I had typed out with each sentence on a separate line.

The Freight Trains

At the train station there are many different freight trains.

They carry 3 kinds of freight across the United States: lumber, vegetables, and coal.

Each train has at least 1 yellow lumber car, 1 green vegetable car, and 1 black coal car.

Each train always has 12 freight cars.

There are never more than 10 cars of one kind.

Freight cars that are the same are always connected.

How many different ways of making trains with 12 cars can you find?

I revealed one line of the problem at a time and we discussed the details. When I was confident they understood what each line meant, I introduced them to the KWC form and explained how we would use it to organize the information in the problem. I asked them to write down in the appropriate spaces what they Knew, what they Wanted to find, and any special Conditions (rules) they had to keep in mind. After a few minutes, I asked individuals to share what they had written, and I wrote their answers on a class KWC transparency. Students who had overlooked pieces of information were able to add the missed parts to their own copies. The completed KWC looked like this:

K What do you know for sure?	**W** What do you want to find out?	**C** Are there any special conditions? (Special rules? Tricks to watch out for? Things to remember?)
I know that: • there are many different trains • each train has 12 cars	I'm trying to: • find out how many different trains can have 12 cars	I need to remember: • freight cars of the same kind have to be connected • there are never more than 10 of the same kind of car • each train has some of each kind of car (coal, lumber, vegetables)

Prior to the lesson, I had prepared several Unifix-cube trains to test their understanding of the problem's conditions. They were quickly able to tell me which trains were acceptable and explain in what way(s) the unacceptable ones didn't follow the rules. I also handed out a paper with four acceptable "trains" already built. I told them that when they had built a train they felt fit all the criteria, they should raise their hands. After I had checked their work, they could record each train on paper using colored pencils or crayons.

After students had worked for about fifteen minutes, most partners had completed and recorded their first three or four trains. I modeled how to record with numbers the count of each type of car in the train. I asked students to name one combination of numbers that they used. One pair identified 4, 4, 4. I asked if any other students had also built a 4, 4, 4 train. Several offered this combination with the colors in a different order, which I displayed near the first in the pocket chart. It was fortuitous that this combination was named first, because children very willingly agreed that regardless of the order, any train that was 4, 4, and 4 had the same number of each kind of car. Which cars were in the front, middle, and back made no difference. They already knew the commutative property of addition through "turnaround" facts and were now introduced to the idea that the same held true even if there were three addends. I said this idea was called the *associative property* without making a big deal of the new vocabulary term. They agreed to group all the 4, 4, 4 combinations behind the first one, and I wrote 4 + 4 + 4 on an index card. This procedure was repeated with different combinations of cars totaling 12. Many children found the same combinations in the same order, while others found the same numbers in different sequences. After this first round, students had found eight different number combinations.

I told them they to try to make more trains in combinations that were not already displayed in the pocket chart. Several groaned after building what they proudly thought was a new combination only to find it was already on the board with addends in a different order, but none were dissuaded to the point of giving up. They were determined to find a combination no one else had yet discovered. They worked for about ten minutes more before we stopped to record their newest additions to our pocket chart. Four additional combinations were found, bringing the class total to 12.

My final series of questions centered on whether or not we had accomplished what the problem had challenged us to do—find *all* the combinations. Some quickly responded, "Yeah! There are 12 cars and we found all 12 ways." I asked whether the problem told us there were 12 ways. Most of the kids agreed that we had no way of knowing if 12 ways were all the ways there were. "How do we know if we found all the ways?" I asked. No one had a good suggestion for how to know for sure until I reminded them of previous combination problems we had done (such as finding all the outfits that could be made with 3 shirts and 3 pairs of pants). They remembered that in the outfit problem we had started with 1 pair of pants and put each shirt with it before moving on to the next pair of pants. One of the students finally suggested we could put the numbers in order to see if we had found them all.

Because the problem limited the number of one type of car to 10 we began there. They knew that there could not be a 10, 2, 0 train since there had to be at least one of each kind of car on each train. I recorded 10, 1, 1 on the whiteboard and turned the corresponding index card in the pocket chart around to the blank side to show that we had accounted for that one. Moving down, students discovered the only combination with 9 was 9, 2, 1. A train with 8 of one kind led to two combinations—8, 2, 2 and 8, 3, 1. We continued to add to the list (and turn over the corresponding index cards in the pocket chart) finding two combinations having 7 as an addend, three that had an addend of 6, and two having 5 as an addend. When we got down to 4 as the first addend, the children realized that the other cars had to total 8. However, we had already listed 7, 4, 1, as well as 6, 4, 2 and 5, 4, 3, on our list. Children knew we had to write 4, 4, 4 and felt we had completed our ordered list as we turned over the last index card in the pocket chart.

To be sure, I asked again if we had found all of the combinations. "What happens if we continue our list with combinations that start with 3? How many other cars go with 3 to make a train of 12?" When they answered, "9," I followed up with, "What number pairs can make 9?" The children realized that all the combinations of 9 (8 and 1, 7 and 2, 6 and 3, and

5 and 4) had already been included in our list with 3 as the third addend. Convinced of their success on the problem, the children erupted in cheers. They had enjoyed the experience!

This was a very successful lesson. The children, even those for whom math was usually drudgery, were highly engaged and focused clearly on the task and its many conditions. They showed a conceptual understanding of the associative property (while not necessarily knowing the term) by being able to identify which of their combinations matched a previously offered combination that had the same addends in a different order. They communicated precisely with me and one another when talking about the facts, the task, and the conditions included in the problem as well as while building the trains and subsequently organizing their work in the pocket chart and on the ordered list of addends. I was proud of their efforts and their perseverance.

We will revisit the language issues raised in this chapter in several other chapters. We have deliberately focused on establishing a culture in the early grades where discourse is a valued part of doing the mathematics. Amy focused on math talk and brought her second graders along in a very intentional manner. Julie chose an activity that many elementary school teachers have told me is much too hard for second graders to do. Her second graders rose to the challenge. The freight train problem depends upon the students discussing with one another what is going on. Julie skillfully used the KWC to organize their work and understand each part of the process. Deanna had taught kindergarteners and first graders before tackling second graders. She was confident because she knew what the process of collaboration and discourse required of these youngsters.

How Asian Languages Facilitate Learning Numbers and Operations

In 1987, psychologist Irene Miura found that "in Asian languages . . . place value is inherent in the number language"—speakers will count "ten, ten-one, ten-two . . . two tens." These languages greatly facilitate regrouping and renaming in computation. Miura also found that the concept of fractional parts is inherent in the words used: "one third" would be said as *san bun no ichi*, literally, "of three parts, one." Speakers of Asian languages showed "greater flexibility for mental number manipulation" than their U.S. counterparts (Miura 2001). Without this linguistic advantage, U.S. teachers have an even greater need to provide students many verbal experiences with number relationships.

CHAPTER

3

Broadening the Definition of Problem Solving

IN THE PAST, problem solving in mathematics was considered to be a task in which students applied what they had been taught. Students read a "story problem" (often a thinly disguised computational exercise); determined whether to add, subtract, multiply, or divide; and calculated the answer. For example: "Paco bought 20 apples yesterday at the supermercado. He and Juan ate 12 of them. How many does he have left?"

What Problem Solving Has Been: Story Problems

In her book, *A Man Left Albuquerque Heading East,* Susan Gerofsky (2004) provides us with a history of story problems that goes back not hundreds but thousands of years. Scholars of antiquities have discovered story problems on many clay tablets of Babylonian origin circa 2000 B.C., on the Rhind Papyrus from Egypt circa 1560 B.C., and in the writings of the Qin Dynasty in China circa 300 B.C. Similar story problems have been found in ancient and medieval India, medieval Europe, and the Islamic world. One can follow a continuous record of similar story problems from early Renaissance Europe to the present. Here are two golden oldies. The first is from Alcuin of York, advisor to Charlemagne, circa 780 A.D.:

> A man had to cross a river with a wolf, a goat, and a cabbage. The only boat he could find could only take 2 of them at a time. He had been told that the 3 items must be delivered in good condition. How could this be done?

The second is from Renaissance Italy:

> The Holy Father sent a courier from Rome to Venice commanding that he should reach Venice in 7 days. And the Signoria of Venice sent another courier to Rome, telling him that he must reach Rome in 9 days. From Rome to Venice is 250 miles. The couriers left at the same time. In how many days will they meet, and how many miles will each have traveled?

Dozens of versions of each of these have circulated the globe.

Gerofsky considers mathematical story problems to be a linguistic and literary *genre* that is thoroughly embedded in the math curriculum and in its pedagogy. As a genre, story problems have their own text structure. Gerofsky outlines a "constellation of features" that co-occur in story problems. For instance, she notes "unusual forms of reference, an anomalous use of verb tense, and a particular discourse structure" (Gerofsky 2004, 4–5). People in these problems have no background or reality other than the hypothetical or imaginary world of the particular story problem. The verbs are often conditional or subjunctive and even arbitrary, lacking the consistency of standard prose.

These problems have a three-component, ordered structure consisting of

- a setup that establishes the setting, the context, the situation, the characters, and so on—a component that is not essential to the mathematics of the problem
- information needed to solve the problem and often some irrelevant information to distract the solver
- a question.

Gerofsky makes the conjecture that thousands of years ago story problems were a fairly sensible method of teaching the next generation of merchants, traders, and builders of their societies the mathematics they needed to know. Some of these story problems were practical applications of math to real-life settings. Others were fanciful, whimsical, and unrealistic. The first component (the context) was virtually irrelevant mathematically and could be changed to make the problem more interesting or amusing and, therefore, more memorable (i.e., instead of Alan buying cupcakes at the bakery, we find Paco buying apples at the supermercado). Students of the day completed dozens of these problems (and much more challenging ones involving square roots!) deriving or practicing a standard algorithm for a particular type of problem.

Gerofsky notes that this may have been useful before the introduction of algebra since there was no way to show the generalized method for doing the calculations of the types of problems confronting the merchants of Venice. Without generalizable formulas, people had to explain each step in language and give many numerical examples of how to calculate an answer. Why didn't the rise of algebra as a major tool circa 1400 A.D. cause the decline of story problems? Given algebra's power to generalize through the use of variables, expressions, and equations, why would particular numerical algorithms need to be memorized? Gerfosky believes that rather than repudiating story problems as no longer needed, their proponents justified them as practical applications of mathematics.

I can remember story problems proliferating in algebra texts thirty to fifty years ago. The problems were grouped together and taught by type. Each type of problem had its own peculiar algorithm to get the right answer. The problems dealt with mixed nuts, 2 trains, a boat on a river with a current, mixed solutions, 2 people working on a task alone or together, and others that I have repressed. The algorithms were memorized or applied without regard for understanding the concepts inherent in the situation. This practice of grouping problems by type was discouraged in the original NCTM Standards in 1989.

Story problems are justified as useful today even though research studies have shown "practical, applied mathematics in work situations are often quite different from word-problem forms and solution methods taught in schools" (Gerofsky 2004, 131). She further noted that elementary school teachers "valued practical, contextualized, open-ended problems over abstractly mathematical ones" (135).

Problem Solving Beyond the Traditional

How can we do better than the story problems of yesteryear? Attacking good problems is not an application of what students have already learned; it is the major vehicle for building new meaning. Every lesson within every math period—even skill building—should be reconceived as problem solving. Forget about the problem of the week. Help the students see the patterns that are everywhere every day.

Choosing Good Problems

Using practical, contextualized, open-ended problems starts with finding problems, tasks, or activities that:

- are set in easily imaginable, real-world situations
- are set in intriguing contexts or have inherently interesting, motivating premises that provoke students to think

- contain rich, deep, meaningful mathematics, big ideas, and important concepts that can be understood and connected to related concepts.

Student-Generated Problems

What would make a problem "practical"? Perhaps the problem stems from questions that the students pose. There are several excellent articles and books on problem posing by students in mathematics (see, for instance, Brown and Walter [1990, 1993]). One of the simplest ways for students to generate interesting extensions is to ask them to deliberately change one of the aspects of the K, the W, or the C in a problem they have just completed. The KWC is a metacognitive prompt described in the Introduction.

Think about inquiry in science, which is ideally generated by the students. It often starts with "I wonder" and continues with posters covering the Wonder Wall with questions, many of which can be readily transformed into math problems. Similarly in social studies, there is inquiry about geographic-political-social-economic issues that could be framed mathematically. Hurricane tracking, the Olympics, or the Iditarod Trail Sled Dog Race are obvious events of mathematical interest. Carol Greenes and her colleagues (1989) produced two decks of one hundred cards each that describe in a paragraph some "amazing facts and real problems." The final line of each card poses a question to be answered. We can simply omit that question and let the students pose their own question.

> The brontosaurus, a giant, lizard-like dinosaur, lived about 190 million years ago. It was about 75 feet long from its nose to the end of its tail. Its neck was 20 feet long. Its footprints were 36 inches long and 26 inches wide. The brontosaurus weighed about 30 tons. Because it was so large and heavy, the brontosaurus traveled very slowly, not more than 4 miles per hour, which is about the walking speed of an adult human. Today, the largest land animal is the African elephant. It can grow to be about 25 feet long and about 13 feet tall. The African elephant may weigh as much as 16,500 pounds.

Can you generate some good questions that are based on this factual information? The card asked: "About how many African elephants together weigh the same as 1 brontosaurus? (answer: 4)." The question determines the degree of difficulty of the mathematics involved. When you encourage students to formulate the question, you are showing your trust in them to make sensible questions.

Open-Ended Problems

There is not a single correct answer to an open-ended problem. There might be many answers, as in a problem in which students have to figure out all the possible combinations of a set of objects or elements. I don't give them a formula for finding the number of combinations, but instead they must construct and record each combination in order to see the patterns emerging.

Pam Regan, a third-grade teacher (now a principal) in the River Forest (Illinois) School District, has her students determine the different pizzas that can be made with a variety of toppings. The students get very excited about the possibilities and the patterns that they find.

I hand my students paper plates (or paper circles) that represent pizza dough, one per child. The kids color the paper with red crayon to represent the tomato sauce. Next they add the cheese, represented by a paper circle with jagged edges, which the kids color with yellow crayons. At this point, they each have a standard cheese pizza with no toppings.

Then I have them create paper versions of 5 different toppings: green peppers, pepperoni, onions, bacon, and mushrooms. Their task is to determine how many ways these ingredients can be combined on a pizza. Only a few of my students can use abstract symbols to code the various combinations, but by creating physical representations I hope they will see the patterns that emerge.

When everyone has created a pizza, I call the class together. "Did anyone keep the standard cheese pizza with no toppings?" Anticipating that no one will have, I have kept 1 aside. "How many of you used only 1 topping for your pizza?" Only 2 kids have. When they hold up their pizzas, I make a big deal of the fact that they each have different single toppings. "In how many ways is it possible to have a pizza with only 1 topping? We have 2 ways now. What are the other ways?" I call on several kids, who suggest the 3 remaining ingredients. We quickly determine there are only 5 ways to use only 1 of the 5 toppings.

Now I ask how many students used 2 toppings; 6 students have. "Did you each make a different combination? Do we have any duplicates? Are any the same?" (This is a key question for combination problems.) There is a duplication: 2 kids created a pepperoni-and-onion pizza. "That leaves 5 different combinations with 2 toppings. We also found 5 ways to have a pizza with 1 topping. Is this the pattern or are there more ways we need to look for?" Several students say there are more than 5 ways to combine 2 toppings and they give examples.

To help them "see" what they have done and think of other alternatives, I have prepared a gigantic poster from a roll of butcher paper, 15 × 3 feet, on which they can display their pizzas. The students with unique topping combinations glue their pizzas on the poster under the appropriate heading, and I choose one of the students with identical pizzas to glue on his or hers. Then I have the students create pizzas with new combinations. We work our way through the possible combinations until we reach the 5-toppings-on-1-pizza option.

Figure 3.1 shows the remarkable pattern my third graders uncovered. They saw the 1-5-10-10-5-1 pattern in the number of possible combinations of toppings. They also discovered that if they kept 1 of the toppings constant, it helped them figure out the others. One little genius saw, in her own words, "how the answers paired up." The 2 "ends" (0 and 5 toppings) have only 1 way: you have to use none of the 5 or all 5 toppings. Then 1 and 4 toppings "are like opposites. If you have a mushroom as your 1, somewhere you must have only the other 4 toppings. It's the same with 2 and 3 toppings. If you have pepperoni and onion for your 2 toppings, then its opposite, mushroom, green pepper, and bacon, will be in the 3-topping bunch." She had noticed the inverse relationship.

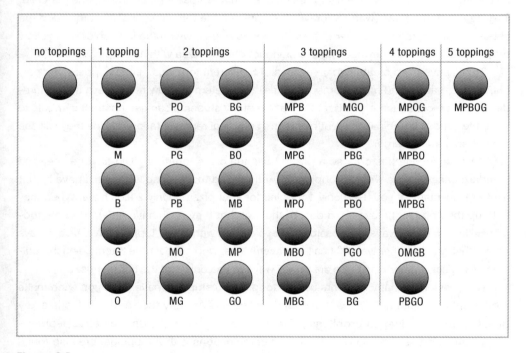

Figure 3.1

Figure 3.2 shows the 3-toppings section of the chart. I didn't push my students to create a traditional organized list. Instead, I let the children think about how to code these pizzas. Realizing that G O and O G are the same pizza or that any one of the 3-topping pizzas could be coded in 6 different orders (M-B-O, M-O-B, O-M-B, O-B-M, B-M-O, and B-O-M) was sufficiently significant.

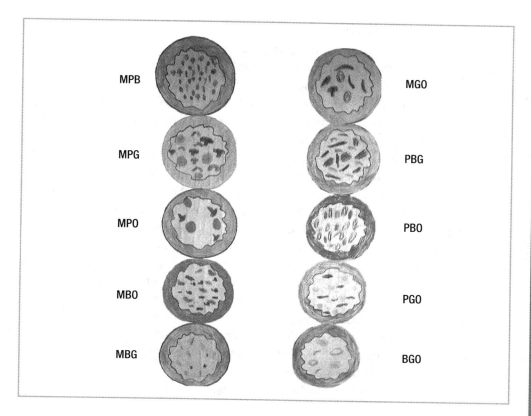

Figure 3.2

When Pam chose to do this combination problem, she had to think through a number of tricky issues. Only a few of her students would be able to generate a symbolic list. However, she was fairly certain that if they had some manipulatives they could make solutions and then label or code them in some way. Making a giant poster gave the kids the additional visual information to help them organize their solutions as data.

Situated Cognition

Situated cognition refers to learning and problem solving in a particular context. In real life, people often develop specific types of mathematics to handle specific needs. These ways of thinking about the concepts and accompanying procedures make perfect sense to those who use them but bear little resemblance to the mathematics typically learned in school. People who use mathematics extensively in their work (carpenters, architects, rocket scientists) organize their ways of thinking mathematically around situations and problems, not around abstractions in math textbooks. They often use shorthand methods that apply only to them.

For instance, a newspaper reported on page 1 (on February 2, 2002) that a foot of heavy, wet snow was dumped on Chicago and people should be careful shoveling. To calculate the weight of snow on a driveway, they used a procedure: the weight of the snow in pounds equals the length (in feet) times the width (in feet) of the driveway times the height of the snow (in inches) times 0.575. What! Where did the 0.575 come from? It is a shortcut that will work for any heavy, wet snow, which weighs 6.9 pounds per cubic foot. First, we convert the height of the snow from inches to feet by multiplying by 0.0833 ($\frac{1}{12}$). Multiplying this number by the length and width of the driveway would give us the volume of snow in cubic feet—but the shortcut goes one step further by including the 6.9 pounds for us: $0.575 = 6.9 \times 0.0833$. So we need to multiply only by the one factor of 0.575, instead of the two original factors. This gives a general procedure that would work whatever the height of the snow.

The Importance of Context

The previous snow example is just one example of math used in a particular context. Children first come to understand a concept in a specific context or situation. This initial understanding is grounded in a set of specific examples. It is not yet a broad understanding that can be generalized to other contexts.

Young students' knowledge is generally organized around their experiences, not around the abstract concepts of the discipline of mathematics as the knowledge of an expert mathematician would be. Working in a meaningful context can help children develop an initial understanding of a concept. By working with several examples of the concept in the same context, individual students inductively derive patterns that create a particular, context-specific version of the concept.

Conceptual understanding is not an on-off light switch: We don't understand a concept in an all-or-nothing way. Initially we grasp some aspect of the concept and build on it, adding and elaborating our understanding. I think of it as building a snowman. First, we find some good snow—not too wet and slushy, not too dry and powdery. We make a snowball with our hands and roll it in the good snow we've found. The ball gains size as more snow sticks to it. We make a big, sturdy ball of snow for the foundation. We repeat this process for the other parts of the snowman. But we must continue to roll the snowball in the right kind of snow; rolling it in the wrong snow—or worse, on grass—will not accumulate more snow. In general, the more connections of the right kind we make, the more examples in different but relevant contexts we encounter, the more elaborate the networks of ideas and relationships we develop, the deeper, richer, more generalized, and more abstract our understanding of a concept becomes.

Only after the students have intellectually wrestled with the problem in context will a cogent explanation of the concept be effective. *Now* we can tailor our explanations to the *students'* conceptions. We can help them *connect* the mathematical concepts directly to what they have just done, just expressed, just realized. We explicitly build bridges between ideas, the new and the known. We explicitly make connections between and among concepts. We help students *crystallize* their understanding.

Solving Similar Problems in Many Contexts

Once students have begun to understand a concept in one context, we begin to help them transfer that understanding to new contexts and tease out the general mathematical principles that are independent of context. For example, most children who have experienced very cold winter weather have a tentative, initial understanding of the concept of negative numbers; they know that temperature is measured on a thermometer (a vertical number line) that includes negative numbers. We can use this initial expression of the concept to fill in any gaps in their knowledge of below-zero temperatures, but we cannot assume students can transfer this knowledge to another context (below par in golf, for example).

We therefore carefully select, from among several options, a second context in which students can develop the concept of negative numbers. We introduce "bridging activities" that help students strip away contextual attributes that are extraneous to understanding the concept and focus on the similarities in the two contexts. For example, we could compare altitude (above and below sea level) and temperature (above and below zero). Both can be displayed vertically on a number line. It may take three or four different contexts, each developed with a half-dozen examples, before students are able to generalize—experience their aha! moment. Textbooks don't devote this kind of time and energy to conceptual development. They supply only a handful of examples in only one context, focusing on generalizing the procedures, not the concepts.

Neg. #s

Representations and Contexts

Figure 3.3 illustrates how we can build experiences for students through varied representations and varied contexts. The diagram may seem complicated; the interactions are complex, and life in the classroom is not simple. Let's start at the top and work down.

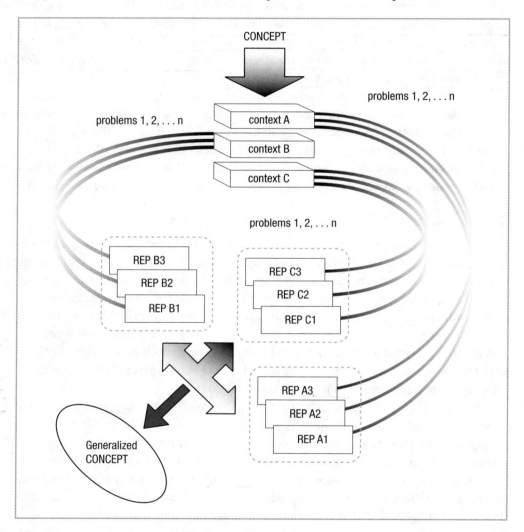

Figure 3.3

We have a concept in mind when we plan a lesson. We decide to have the kids think about context A. The kids work on several problems, creating representations for each one. We debrief with the students after each problem and then, through questions and explanations, attempt to solidify their understanding of the concept *in this context*. (The dotted shapes surrounding the representation groupings represent debriefing).

When we are sure all the students have a good *initial development* of the concept in context A, we introduce a different context (context B) for the concept, again with several problems. We debrief after each problem, highlighting how each problem in this context exemplifies the concept. If the kids don't bring it up first, we ask them to compare and contrast the representations and the meanings of the concept in each context. We then repeat this process with a third context.

Then we encourage the students to strip away all the differences among the three contexts and push for the commonalities. We help them build understanding, guide them toward more abstract representations that are less and less concerned with the particular features of each context. This helps students build a generalized understanding of the concept that can be used in a variety of other contexts.

As a reasonable assessment of how generalized the concept is within a student's knowledge, we can introduce problems in new contexts in which the concept could possibly be used. Can the students make the connection, realizing that the new context contains yet another example of the concept?

Susan Hildebrand teaches third graders in a Title I program in Jenks, Oklahoma. In this story Susan describes how she helped students build their understanding of the concept of multiplication through working with a variety of numbers and representations in one context, then changes the context to help them build a more generalized conception of the patterns of multiplication.

Working in One Context: The Horse Ranch Project

The students arrive at the math room with excitement because they will begin a new "project." Nonfiction and fiction books about horses and ranches are nestled in a tub along with a bucket of pattern blocks and a set of dominos on the check-in table providing a preview of the next project. As the students gather around the table, I tell them: "Our new project begins with a story." I show them a picture to study and think about. "What do you see?" Josh is first to say, "I see horses." "Has anyone ever touched a horse?" Hands are raised. "What color was the horse?" Emily pauses and then blurts out, "It is black." The students have much to share since they are familiar with horses from books, television, and visits to the state fair or to a nearby ranch. Susie shares a story about the horse she once owned with details of the blaze on its face and the black-and-white color of the tail.

The students are intrigued as the new story begins: "Imagine you work on a horse ranch with 24 horses." I tell them, "We can use one of our reading strategies to help us think about our story. Let's use visualization with our story. That's when we see pictures in our brain. Remember, it's like we have a 'movie in our mind.' Think about what those horses look like. Are your 24 horses lined up in a row, or nose to tail, nose to tail? What color are they? Are they all black?"

Everyone has an idea of what the horses look like. Corrie goes in great detail, "10 of mine are white with brown spots, the other 10 are babies, brown with black spots, and other 4 are white newborns." She is able to *unitize* her counting of 24. I guide the students throughout the project, giving them "gift of time," and encouraging them to communicate their thinking.

Students are engaged and listen as I tell the story once again. "Imagine you work on a horse ranch that has 24 horses. The owner of the ranch tells you that you must put all of the horses in corrals." After a pause, I ask, "Does anyone know what *corrals* are?"

I get several answers: "They are little ranches with gates that you put around horses so they don't get out," "made out of wood," and "I saw a picture of one in that book over there." I finish the story, "You can fence off the corrals many different ways. The owner says you must put the same number of horses in each corral. What is one way you might do this? How many different ways to do this can you find?"

"Today, Josh and Luke are new to our math group and have never used a KWC chart before, so let's work together to complete the KWC." While helping Josh and Luke, I know that this will also help the others in the group become more secure and independent with the chart. The KWC chart pulls out elements of the problem while using the "asking questions" reading strategy. "Let's do our KWC now." Emily speaks up "K is for *know*. What do you know for sure?" I reread the story quickly and say, "We are going to look at K. What is something you know for sure from the story?" The list begins: work on a horse ranch, 24 horses, there are corrals. "What about W? What are we trying to find out?" Corrie raises her hand and stands up to answer, "You are trying to figure out how many numbers to put in the corrals." I repeat what she just said emphasizing the word *number*. The students interrupt to say, "Horses in each corral!"

"Let's look at C." I prompt. "Are there any special conditions? What do we know for sure to solve this problem? It is like our checklist." Emily tells us, "We need 24 horses." After Corrie says we need corrals, she adds, "I figured out something about corrals. It has my name in it, CORRA!" "Same number of horses in each corral," adds Josh.

Placing a plastic tub on the table, I explain: "Today in our project kit, we have 24 Unifix cubes and some corrals that are made out of Popsicle sticks. What do you think the Unifix cubes represent if we have 24 cubes?" "The horses!" exclaims Emily. While still at the table, I ask the students to show me one way that they could put the horses in corrals. As they turn and talk to their partner, I hear Josh say, "I got it! We are trying to make all fours."

Wanting to understand his thought, I ask, "What does that look like?" Josh moves the Unifix cubes in and out of the corrals and decides he needs more than 2 corrals to finish the solution. On the other side of the table, Emily and Corrie are busy counting out 6 cubes each. "I'll put 6 here and put another 6 in the same corral. Oh, that's 12 and put these 12 cubes over here. 12 and 12, that's 24!"

Since Emily wants to make sure they have used all 24 cubes, she recounts the cubes by twos. Listening to their conversation, I ask, "What are you thinking about? So, how does that relate to the corrals?" While pointing to 2 corrals, Corrie explains that each cube represents a horse and we put 6 and 6 in each corral, which uses all 24 cubes or horses. Luke adds, "I knew that there would be 2 corrals because 12 plus 12 equals 24."

"You did a great job corralling the horses, but now you need to fill in a sentence strip that describes your corrals and horses." Holding up a sentence strip, I say, "It reads '___ corrals with ___ horses in each corral.' Emily, what would you write in the blanks?" Emily completes the sentence strip as 2 corrals with 12 horses in each corral. "Glue your sentence strip into your math notebook, and make a simple drawing of your cubes and corrals."

I emphasize internalizing the work. I want kids to repeat back the instructions for added reinforcement. I release math partners to work on the carpet or at the table with their project tub, notebook, pencils, and glue sticks.

As I drop in on students' mathematical conversations, they discuss, predict, and process their data. When a student or small group hits a roadblock, I ask simple questions such as, "What does that look like? Can you prove that? What are our special conditions?" The questions help the students revise their thinking in order to further develop understanding. With my notebook in hand, I record what they have said and done—formative assessments that I'll review later.

As I regroup students in our math huddle for debriefing, they share their solutions, which are then listed on a T-chart in a random manner. A second T-chart reorganizes the data in numerical order. The students discover patterns on the second T-chart, such as "I see 1, 2, 3, 4, here and 4, 3, 2, 1 there," "The numbers become larger as they go down the list," "All of the ways make 24," "They are turn around facts," and "The top half of numbers look like the bottom half but just flipped around."

As these connections are being, Luke blurts out, "We are doing times!" After a long pause, Grace tells the class, "The T-chart [reorganized] reminds me of the time line I just made in my classroom about Benjamin Franklin." After continued discussion, I ask the students if they would like to do another project kit. The responses: "It's fun!" "Can we do one now?"

I describe a new task: "Write a persuasive letter to me explaining why you should have another project kit. Be sure to include what you learned from this project to support your answer. Try to use any new vocabulary and any connections you made." Writing in their notebooks cements together all of the elements of the project: the thinking, the language, the maneuvering of the manipulatives, the hand-drawn representations, and the use of symbolic representations. I support the students by front-loading the task, giving them meaningful, rich text, open-ended problems, and providing manipulatives—even some that are real to life. The students become engaged and take ownership of the problem.

Working in Multiple Contexts

After a few days, I introduce several new project kits. The new kits continue the same pattern of the Horse Ranch Project but give the students multiple contexts in which to develop and deepen their conceptual and mathematical thinking. Before releasing the students with their new kit, I give them time to develop the story as we did with the Horse Ranch Project. When assembling a project kit, a "story" is included that has engaging, real-world texts and situations so that the students become an integral part of the solution. The students recognize a name of a friend or teacher or a school club that's purposely placed in the story, catching their attention. I update stories as needed to meet the needs or activities of the students. Multiple contexts for the same concept reinforce those connections and strengthen number sense. Each project has two versions of the story printed on cardstock ($4\frac{1}{4} \times 5\frac{1}{2}$ inches) using appropriate clip art to visually enhance the problem. The first story contains a specific number of items while in the second story the number of items is left blank. This allows for quick differentiation.

1. The Treasure Map

As Nate was riding his bicycle on the trail, he noticed something in an old tree. He had found an old treasure map. Nate followed the map and discovered some gold coins. He found 60 gold coins! He decided to put the coins in bags to carry them home. He needed to put the same number of coins in each bag. What is one way that Nate carried the gold coins home? How many different ways could Nate carry home the gold coins?

The project's story includes the name of one the classmates (Nate). This technique engages students' imagination throughout the story and creates excitement as they complete the KWC chart and find solutions.

As the partners begin working Ricardo tells Jessie, "There could be all 60 in 1 bag. That's an easy one!" They open their notebooks, draw a T-chart, and record their data. "How did you know to make a T-chart in your notebook?" Jessie shares, "That's what we did to keep track of our work with the Horse Ranch Project." Ricardo illustrates where he had labeled his T-chart with "bags" and "coins in a bag." Continuing on, they used 6 bags with 10 cubes. Jessie suggests using 8 bags, "8 will work!" But does it? After moving the

Unifix cubes in and out of bags, they decide to move on and try 2 bags with 30. "Ricardo, have we done this one yet?" He checks his T-chart and tells her, "Not yet." As they continue, they recognize a pattern and include the "opposites" on the T-chart.

As they continue to work, the following conversation is overheard: "Do you think we have them all?" "We need to do another T-chart. This time we'll put them in order including the flip-arounds," replied Ricardo. "We did it! Mrs. Hildebrand, Ricardo and I are done!" Jessie proudly announces as they clean up.

I differentiated by using different numbers for different students. For example, having noticed Jack's difficulty with 42 on a previous project, I gave him the Treasure Map story with 36.

2. Hair Bows for Sale

The After School Club has been making hair bows to sell at the next PTAG meeting. They are raising money to buy extra school supplies. Today, they have 36 hair bows to package for sale. The PTAG president says you must put the same number of hair bows in each package. What is one way you might do this? How many different ways to do this can you find?

Grace was the inspiration for one of our newest projects, "Hair Bows for Sale." Her mother had taught her how to make hair bows, and she wore a different bow each day. Daily the students would ask questions about the newest hair bow and how it was made. The students used this background knowledge to discuss, to visualize the situation, and to comprehend the problem. The project kit for the Hair Bows for Sale project included the story, an assortment of hair bows, Unifix cubes, and display cards. "Can we use the hair bows?" was the first question asked by Grace and Julie. With smiles on their faces, they counted out 36 "real" hair bows ready for packaging to sell. Julie decided they should make 6 packages for the hair bows. When asked why she chose 6, she answered, "I used 6 corrals with the Horse Ranch Project and 6 was a good number." After the hair bows were packaged, both students counted and verified there was the same number in each package.

Julie and Grace understood that they needed to put the same number of hair bows in each package. In their notebooks, they drew pictures of the packages with 6 hair bows in each. They also wrote a sentence describing packages below each picture. As they continued working through the hair bow project, they periodically found a number that didn't work. Once Grace counted by fives and tracked the groups of 5 with her fingers, she announced "5 won't work. Let's try another number."

As the students were finishing their projects, Sarah asked, "Can we name our first T-chart *R* for random and the second one *O* for organized?" She explained that would be a way to keep track of our T-charts. Everyone excitedly agreed that they liked the idea!

3. American Red Cross

Jenks East Elementary third and fourth graders volunteer at the American Red Cross. Today, there are 32 Band-Aids to pack into Red Cross bags. The nurse says you must put the same number of Band-Aids in each bag. What is one way you might do this? How many different ways to do this can you find?

The American Red Cross project is one that both boys and girls enjoy. White sacks labeled with the American Red Cross emblem, Band-Aids, red Unifix cubes, and a story involving the school nurse are packed into the project kit.

4. The Cupcake Shoppe

Mrs. Cronk and Mrs. Hobson have just opened a cupcake shop. They sell only cupcakes. Today's cupcakes are chocolate with pink frosting topped with chocolate sprinkles. They have 48 cupcakes to display in their shop. All of the cupcakes need to be on pink trays. Each pink tray must have the same number of cupcakes. How many different ways to do this can you find?

Can you visualize those cupcakes? Could you or the students make "confectionary connections" with The Cupcake Shoppe? After sharing this problem at a recent professional development class, two of the teachers seriously questioned others, "Did Angela and Susan really start a cupcake business?"

Horses, Hair Bows, and Cupcakes?

So, what do horses, hair bows, and cupcakes have to do with math? Everything! As the students work through different contexts or project kits, they add to their experiences and achieve deeper conceptual understanding. The students make math-to-math connections from their experiences. These experiences take time and the multiple contexts underpin the learning. It is very encouraging to read the "math love notes" received from students (i.e., "Math rocks!" and "I love math!").

Susan aptly demonstrates that when students get a chance to work with the same concept in varied contexts that the teacher debriefs with them, they can build powerful experiences and conceptual understanding. The additional time spent on multiple problems is minimal when compared to the time that would be spent on reteaching.

Rethinking Problem-Solving Strategies

Problem-solving strategies help students interpret problems. When students share these strategies with us, we get an insight into how they are conceiving of a problem. Students' conceptions of a problem are especially important when they are *mathematizing* (using math concepts and appropriate mathematical thinking) a real-world situation. Math textbooks often give teachers and students the misconception that every problem-solving strategy introduced is equally important. However, it is useful to identify three kinds of strategies: metastrategies, representational strategies, and supplementary strategies.

Metastrategies

Metastrategies are intimately connected to any kind of mathematical thinking, and students should always use them and be aware that they are doing so. These include looking for a pattern and using logical reasoning.

Since math is the science of patterns, students should be constantly looking for patterns. When textbooks introduce the look-for-a-pattern strategy, they invariably are teaching a specific pattern, such as odd and even numbers. However, knowing what the pattern is and trying to apply it is *not* what mathematicians do. Instead, they believe a pattern exists (in the data or in nature) but don't know what the pattern is *until they discern it*.

And when students encounter the page explaining the use-logical-reasoning strategy, they would be within their rights to ask, "What have we been doing in math up to now?" Or, "What is the alternative?" Most textbooks illustrate this strategy with a so-called logic problem:

> There are 5 houses on the west side of the street. Mr. White does not live in the white house. Mr. Brown does not live in the brown house. Mr. Green does not live in the green house. Mr. Black does not live in the black house. Mr. Pink does not live in the pink house. The white house and the black house are on the corners of the street.

And so on. After being given additional information about specific houses, students are supposed to determine in which house each person lives and its position on the block. Of course, anyone must use logical reasoning to eliminate some of the options (Mr. White does *not* live in the white house), but the students are asked to make a table, usually called a logic table, in which they enter *yes* or *no* in the appropriate cells. The strategy is really one based on tabular representation.

If you think of a strategy as a method that you consciously choose to use or not use to solve a given problem, then looking for a pattern and using logical reasoning do not fit. These strategies must become habits of mind whenever doing mathematics. Students need to experience different types of reasoning—inductive, deductive, analysis, synthesis—as well as how to discern and interpret patterns. Children need to understand the nuances of the terms when they discuss the ways in which they are thinking about what they are doing, such as the different modes of language described in Chapter 2.

Humans are pattern-seeking, meaning-making creatures. We are so bombarded with sensory stimuli that we have to use this feature of our minds to filter much of the raw sensory input. We can do so by classifying, organizing, sorting, and so on according to familiar patterns. We put things together that share the same attribute(s). We color-code whenever we can. We put things in an order that makes sense to us—numerical, alphabetical, or organizing by size or shape.

Perceiving patterns is essentially an inductive process (going from the particular to the general). A student examines a number of particular examples and derives a pattern. Such perceptions cannot be forced. "Pure" induction, with no feedback or explanation, can be challenging and motivating, especially when the context is conceivable. Some students love the intellectual struggle of wrestling with many examples. However, many students become frustrated and anxious with induction, especially when they are unfamiliar with the context. Teaching is an art—knowing when students are shutting down from frustration or anxiety versus trying to avoid thinking is an on-the-spot decision. Rather than giving an explanation or giving them a procedure to follow, generally a good question directs their focus to something they might have missed.

Conversely, many math teachers require students to work with pure deduction (going from the general to the particular). They explain the rules, formulas, theorems, and principles and then expect the students to apply them to particular situations. The main difficulty with deductive reasoning is that most of the time the explanations we give do not connect to anything in the students' minds. They need to see examples to understand the explanation. Thus it makes sense to provide a wealth of examples and add some explanations as we move through a problem. Let's look at two activities that illustrate a good use of inductive and deductive reasoning.

Jennifer Schramm teaches mathematics at Hinsdale Middle School, in the Hinsdale (Illinois) School District. The activity she discusses below requires almost pure *inductive* thinking; there is plenty of "data" to wrestle with but little explanation. I have been saying for years that I'd like to see more math activities that require inductive thinking. However, the danger is that too much induction without feedback can be very frustrating. Jennifer wisely uses high inductive thinking to motivate these nearly burned-out kids.

My students had given up since spring break. They wanted me to solve the problems for them. They weren't asking for guidance anymore; they wanted answers. I decided to try to motivate them again. I explained that our goal this final quarter was to go back to thinking. I told them I was going to put some numbers on the board, and they needed to figure out the pattern. After I had written the numbers on the board, I would answer only yes-or-no questions.

I listed the numbers 1, 6, 11 on the board. The students thought for sure they had the sequence down and said how easy it was. When I wrote the next number, 4, on the board, the look on their faces was priceless. They immediately rethought the pattern as +5, +5, −7.

After they had each written in their journal, I continued to write numbers on the board one by one, asking them to suggest the next number. They jumped to their feet and shouted numbers at me; everyone wanted to be the one to figure out the pattern. They began whispering ideas back and forth. I hadn't seen this kind of excitement for weeks.

Once the repeating sequence was complete—1, 6, 11, 4, 9, 2, 7, 12, 5, 10, 3, 8, 1, 6 . . .—I told them to write in their journal for two minutes about how they felt about guessing numbers that would fit the pattern and what they thought the pattern might be. What were their general observations of the numbers. Are they big numbers? Little numbers? Positive? Negative? Prime? Composite?

After five more minutes in which they processed information in their table groups, I let them share their guesses of what the pattern might be. After several suggestions (all variations of combinations of +5 and −7), I asked them to share their observations about the numbers. They agreed they were small numbers, all positive, both prime and composite, and ranged from 1 through 12. I asked what sorts of numbers that we deal with every day range from 1 through 12. They suggested shoe sizes, calendars, and clocks. We ruled out shoe sizes fairly quickly, because there are no patterns in shoe sizes. Then we discussed the months of the year; 5-month segments repeat in this pattern if we assign each month the number of its position in the 12-month sequence, but there is no real correlation. Finally we talked about clocks. A student suggested that maybe the pattern jumped every 5 hours. Other students stood up and pointed from the numbers on the board to the numbers on the clock. They saw the correlation!

I passed out versions of a blank paper clock without hands and had them draw the pattern: a line from 1 to 6, then from 6 to 11, then from 11 to 4, until they came back to 1, resulting in the "star polygon" shown in Figure 3.4.

They now had several "representations," each showing something different about the pattern: the numbers (very symbolic and abstract); the clock (very real and concrete); and the picture of the star polygon.

I asked them if there was another way the pattern could be described "not in hours." After some active, excited thinking, they came up with "every 25 minutes." I told them I wanted to see this same kind of excitement for the next two months! They said they were excited because this was "fun math," which gave me cause for thought.

Figure 3.4

The next day I passed out their paper clocks again and had them write about the angles in the star pattern. I was delighted. Every student in my room was actively engaged in solving this problem for sixty minutes over the two-day period. They demonstrated conceptual understanding. They put thought and effort into their journal entries.

Jennifer was correct in her intuition that the students could become invigorated by inductive work. She built suspense and engagement by adding to the pattern in pieces; she encouraged them to write and reflect privately as well as share in public; she provided some scaffolding in the discussion.

Becky Hanselman teaches fourth grade at Sandburg School, in the Wheaton (Illinois) School District. In this vignette she explains how a simple game can provoke good *deductive* reasoning, develop communication skills, encourage the use of mental math, and give a context for work with an open number line.

Many classrooms play some form of Guess My Number, a game in which a student picks a number and the other students ask yes-or-no questions to determine the number. The exercise teaches the class how to process the attributes of numbers and how to communicate the attributes in the form of a question. It also teaches students mathematical logic and deductive reasoning.

In my fourth-grade classroom, I used this activity, a ten-minute oral exercise, to help students learn place value, interact with vocabulary, and problem solve. The activity was effective, but some students struggled with the meaning of math terms such as *multiple of 3* or *prime number*.

As the year progressed, I noticed additional benefits. Using it for short periods of time made every minute count. Practicing vocabulary daily gave students more opportunities to become comfortable with words and their meanings as classmates shared their thinking. Students' mental math abilities became stronger because the students had to hold numbers in their head and formulate questions to narrow numbers down. The activity gave me a natural place to help students begin to use a number line to keep track of numbers and see possible answers. Finally, students learned to ask more meaningful questions and thus needed fewer clues to discover the number.

The game rules and procedures I used were:

- Either I or a student chooses a number. The chooser must know the attributes of the number. (I start with a one- or two-digit number to help establish the rules and ensure success; then I move to larger numbers, fractions, and decimals.)

- Students ask yes-or-no questions about the attributes of the number (whole/rational, odd/even, number of digits, etc.).

- Students may not guess numbers until they can prove the answer with the clues.

- Initially I lead the activity. I may prepare cards that guide students' (especially reluctant speakers') questions.

- Every student must ask at least one question.

- All students must record possible answers on a whiteboard.

- After the game is established, I let a student lead while I record the clues. (I know the number.)

- When the game is very familiar, I give students autonomy and observe, assessing their mathematical understanding of number.

- In the interest of time, I may limit the number of questions asked.

- When students are very comfortable asking questions and using the vocabulary appropriately, I let them play it in small groups or pairs so there is more engagement.

The first time my class and I played the game, I didn't give many directions; I wanted to see how much they knew. I asked the students to guess my number (58) using only yes-or-no questions. I got: "Is the number 25?" "Is the number 368?" "Is the number 43?" It became a guessing game. Each question elicited only one piece of information. After a couple of minutes, I asked whether guessing numbers helped them narrow the options. I suggested broader yes-or-no questions such as, "Is the number odd?"

Students quickly learned to begin the game with questions about the attributes of the number: the number of digits, even or odd, divisible by 3. Questions like these narrow down the choices quickly. The quieter students needed prompting at first, so I gave them questions to help them feel comfortable. We moved quickly from two-digit to three-digit numbers. The students were good at seeing how a number fit or didn't fit the clues and could point out their reasoning to their classmates.

Following is an example of a typical session.

Number being guessed: 359

Is it odd? **Yes**

Is it a whole number? **Yes**

Is it a 3-digit number? **Yes**

Is it divisible by 3? **No**

Are all the digits odd? **Yes**

Is it between 300 and 350? **No**

Is it between 300 and 360? **Yes**

Is the ones digit between 0 and 5? **No**

Up to this point, the questions narrow the possibilities. It's an odd number, a whole number, a 3-digit number, not divisible by 3. Discovering that all the digits are odd reduces the possibilities significantly: every digit is 1, 3, 5, 7, 9 (not just the ones digit). "Is it between 300 and 350?" could have narrowed the number had the answer been yes; the no answer only eliminates 15 possibilities. Next Max asks, "Is it between 300 and 360?" Before I answer Molly says, "We just asked a very similar question. We won't get much information from it." But my yes answer shrinks the pool of possibilities to 5. Now the students need to figure out the number.

Jon suggests 351.

Sam states, "It can't be 351 because 351 is divisible by 3. 3 + 5 + 1 = 9, which is divisible by 3, so 351 is divisible by 3."

Grant pipes in, "What about 357? All the digits are odd. It is between 350 and 360. The ones digit is between 5 and 9."

Molly says, "It's divisible by 3: $3 + 5 + 7 = 15$, which can be divided by 3, so it can't be 357."

Suzy says, "I think it's 359 because all the digits are odd. It's between 350 and 360. The ones digit is more than 5, and $3 + 5 + 9 = 17$, which is not divisible by 3."

Number found!

For students to choose a number and lead the game, they had to know the attributes of the number in order to answer the yes-or-no questions correctly. At first I asked the student to whisper the number to me so I could guide the answers. After we played the game for a couple of weeks, I eliminated this safety net, to better assess their knowledge of number attributes.

On one occasion, Alice, a quiet, average math student, walked timidly up to the whiteboard to lead the game. As she called on students to ask questions, another student recorded the answers on the whiteboard.

Melody asked, "Is it even?" Alice softly answered, "Yes."

Mel asked, "Is the number 3 digits?" Very timidly Alice said yes.

Dale inquired, "Is it divisible by 3?" After ten seconds, Alice meekly said no.

Then Sara asked, "Is it divisible by 4?" "Um, uh, yes," Alice replied.

The students continued asking questions until they had these clues:

- even number

- 3-digit number

- not divisible by 3

- divisible by 4

- no repeating digits

- 1 is in the hundreds place

- 4 is in the ones place

- 1 to 5 not in the tens place

Now they began the process of elimination. The students assumed the tens digit had to be more than 5 and narrowed the choices to 164 and 184. Alice smiled as the students reviewed the clues and discovered that both numbers fit. Now came the defining question: "Is the tens digit a 6?" Alice said no.

Greg said triumphantly, "Is the number 184?" Alice confidently repeated no.

The class began to murmur. Finally Grant (a very strong math student) said, "Your clues must be wrong because those are the only possibilities."

"Are you sure it's divisible by 4?" Molly questioned. Alice redid the division mentally and said yes.

Unable to think of any other questions, the class asked, "So what's the number?"

Alice said, "104."

The class gave a loud groan: 104 fit every clue. Alice went back to her seat with a spring in her step, her head held high, and a smile on her face. An average math student had successfully stumped the class with a fairly easy number! The students were so accustomed to using the digits 1 to 9, they forgot about the digit 0. Sometimes we make assumptions that lead to the wrong answer and cloud our ability to see all the options. From then on, the students remembered to ask if there was a 0 in the number.

The game also revealed a great teaching opportunity. When I began using two-digit numbers, I would draw a simple number line to demonstrate the possible numbers. For example, if the number was 73 and the clues so far revealed that it was odd, between 50 and 100, and not divisible by 5, I drew a number line on the board with 50 at one end and 100 at the other. I then took out all the fives and even numbers and crossed off more numbers as the guessing proceeded. When the students had gotten comfortable using this tool, I made the number line more abstract, not including every possible number. I wanted the students to create an image of an empty number line in their head that they would be able to use during math computation and math reasoning. The game helped the students begin to visualize an extensive number line.

Guess My Number can easily be adapted to primary grades. Start first with numbers from 0 to 10 and suggest questions to ask ("Is it even?" for example). Write down all the possibilities and erase the numbers as the clues begin to whittle down the choices. As the students become more comfortable, use numbers to 30. If the class becomes fluent asking questions and proving the number, keep adding additional groups of ten all the way to 100. Let students lead the activity during each progression. Slowly focus on the most important part of the game—the number attributes. Asking the questions, proving the answer, and challenging other students is a meaningful activity that helps lay a strong foundation early on.

Becky uses a simple game to illustrate what deductive thinking ought to be. A student selects a concept that can be used to distinguish among numbers and inquires if that concept pertains to the target number. It is analogous to hypothesis testing. The question should allow for the elimination of nonexamples of the concept. Both the questioner and the one who has chosen the target number must have a good grasp of a wide variety of concepts. The question moves the thinkers from the general to the particular.

Representational Strategies

The second type of problem-solving strategies are *representational strategies* based on how humans process information. They include:

- discussing the problem in small groups (language representations using the aural sense)
- manipulating objects (concrete, physical representations using the tactile sense)
- acting it out (representations of sequential actions using the kinesthetic sense)
- drawing a picture, diagram, or graph (pictorial representations using the visual sense)
- making a list or table (symbolic representations often using abstract reasoning leading to equations).

When students use these strategies, they are creating meaning by interpreting the situation or context of the problem. They can begin to understand the trade-offs that occur with different representations. We may require them to use certain representations to help them build conceptual bridges between representations that become increasingly abstract.

From Concrete to Abstract Representations

Note the dynamic flow from the most concrete to the most abstract representation. Language is used throughout this continuum as students describe what they have done or seen.

I regularly hear this complaint from teachers: "My students can figure out the answer by using manipulatives, but when I try to get them to write out the number sentence as an equation, they can't do it!" Figure 3.5 shows why. These teachers are asking students to go from the most concrete representation to the most abstract in one fell swoop! There are plenty of mediating steps students could take—each with full understanding. Math programs that refer to three levels—concrete, representational, and abstract—mislead teachers into thinking there are only three steps to take. They are all representations (concrete representations and abstract representations); some are more abstract than others.

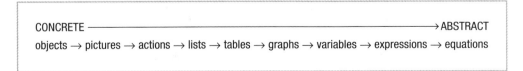

Figure 3.5

When students create meaning using these strategies, they are able to express the mental model they have created; they are building their understanding of the problem. They may or may not find a solution with their first attempt to represent it, but understanding the problem is the first thing they must do. Each successive representation, especially when the modality changes, reveals different concepts or patterns.

Supplementary Strategies

The third type of problem-solving strategies is labeled *supplementary strategies*; students cannot use them effectively unless they understand the problem. They include:

- working backward
- substituting a simpler problem
- guessing and checking.

In order to be able to work backward, students must realize that the problem consists of a sequence of actions. In order to substitute a simpler problem, students must understand what the problem requires (not just use smaller numbers, as students are prone to do). Guessing and checking requires that students know how to check their guess. A wild guess probably can't be checked. Checking for reasonableness is a great idea, but it still requires understanding how to generate a possible solution. Supplementary strategies are best used after students have gained a good understanding of the problem via representational strategies.

Much has been written about problem solving and mathematical thinking. I have chosen to address math modeling as a separate and noteworthy special kind of problem solving that may be our best chance of accomplishing conceptual understanding. In the next chapter, we will look at the possibility of students, even first graders, creating mathematical models.

CHAPTER

4

Mathematical Modeling and Problem Solving

The definition of problem solving posed here is based on the meaning of mathematical modeling, where problem solvers are required to create mathematical ways of thinking about a new situation for some purpose (e.g., to accommodate to new knowledge and/or new technologies, to make sense of complex systems, to make decisions or predictions). A modeling perspective emphasizes students learning mathematics through problem solving and learning problem solving through creating mathematical models.
—Richard Lesh and Judith Zawojewski (2006)

LESTER AND KEHLE (2003) STATE that math problem solving is much more complex than previously thought. It involves knowledge acquisition and use, executive control, affects and beliefs, and a host of contextual factors. They note that "far too little is known about students' learning in mathematically rich environments" (510).

For many years, problem solving has been separated from the learning of mathematical concepts. "However, problem solving is part of what it means to understand a mathematical idea, and thus both learning a mathematical idea and problem solving require interpreting, representing, and reflecting on situations mathematically. By emphasizing the synergistic relationship between learning and problem solving, problem solving is viewed as developing productive ways of interpreting situations (e.g., givens, goals, possible solution processes), i.e., dealing with *mathematical models*" (Lesh and Zawojewski 2006, 770). They underscore "the importance of considering problem-solving processes as embedded in, and linked to, the content of the situation, rather than existing as a stand-alone skill." (2006, 777)

Lesh and Zawojewski state their definition of a problem as:

> A task, or goal-directed activity, becomes a problem (or problematic) when the "problem solver" (which may be a collaborating group of specialists) needs to develop a more productive way of thinking about the given situation. (2006, 798)

For Lesh's researchers, the collaborating groups are usually three middle school students, and a more productive way of thinking means that they must be involved in the process of interpreting the situation mathematically via a "series of express-test-revise cycles to sort out, integrate, modify, revise, and/or refine clusters of mathematical concepts from various topics within mathematics. An interpretation is mathematical if the description or explanation focuses on structural characteristics of the situation." (2006, 799)

The Modeling Perspective

Since the millennium, a substantial number of university researchers have called for a dramatic shift in the way educators view problem solving. They have become disenchanted with the inherent limitations in the traditional approach to problem solving, and they have proposed as an alternative a comprehensive perspective that sees problem solving as modeling. Mathematical modeling has been a staple for engineers, architects, and related professions for many years. It can be seen pervasively in the high school part of the CCSSM content standards.

Even elementary students can create mathematical models. Lehrer and Schauble (2002) report on a study that engaged elementary students from eight classrooms in grades 1 to 5 in the creation of mathematical models that would function as classification systems. They found that young students were indeed able to develop and represent mathematical models and illustrate their findings. Even first and second graders were able to do data-modeling activities. The children collected data on such diverse phenomena as fruit fly dispersion, traffic patterns, recycling, and changes in shadows during the day. Students created their own notation systems, diagrams, experience-based analogies, and other media to express their conceptions. They described and explained their interpretations of the relationships in the phenomena under study. See Lehrer and Schauble (2002), *Investigating Real Data in the Classroom: Expanding Children's Understanding of Math and Science.*

Model Development

Richard Lesh and thirty colleagues collaborated on *Beyond Constructivism: Models and Modeling Perspectives on Mathematics Problem Solving, Learning and Teaching* (Lesh and Doerr 2003b), a comprehensive book demonstrating a significantly different basis not only for problem solving but also for K–16 school mathematics.

Multiple Embodiments

Lesh and his colleagues credit their approach to the work of the brilliant mathematics educator Zoltan Dienes in the 1960s. One of Dienes' ideas was the notion of *embodiments*, which are "concrete manipulatable materials . . . that are useful props to help children develop elementary-but-powerful constructs that provide powerful foundations for elementary mathematical reasoning" (Lesh and Doerr 2003a, 37). Reflective abstraction from physical and mental actions on concrete materials helps students see and understand mathematical relationships.

Dienes (1960) proposed four instructional principles governing the use of embodiments:

1. The *construction principle* posits that the concrete materials support activities in which students develop abstract concepts by performing a series of conceptual actions on the materials, not from the materials themselves. For example, pattern blocks have six different color-coded geometric shapes that children can play with indefinitely without ever realizing the conceptual potential. However, when their "play" is mediated by an adult familiar with such concepts, the children's conceptual actions on the blocks will yield enormous conceptual understanding.

2. The *multiple embodiment principle* holds that for children to go beyond thinking *with* a particular construct or concept to also thinking *about* it, they must consider several structurally similar embodiments. They must go beyond examining a single embodiment to consider the relationships among several embodiments. By varying the contexts, situations, and frames in which the same structures occur, learners can abstract structural and conceptual mathematical similarities. This principle relates directly to the idea of multiple contexts we discussed in the previous chapter (e.g., horse corrals, hair bows, cupcakes, etc.).

3. The *dynamic principle* states that many mathematical concepts, constructs, or conceptual systems involve dynamic operations and transformations. They are not static entities. Therefore students must look for patterns and regularities across embodiments rather than at singular bits of information about attributes and characteristics. Consider all the possibilities of equivalent fractions in their different embodiments that would be necessary for students to experience as they construct their conceptual understanding.

4. The *perceptual variability principle* maintains that every embodiment has some features that are not part of the abstract conceptual system, as well as that every abstract system has some characteristics the embodiment does not have. Therefore, students need to investigate embodiments with different perceptual characteristics. For example, many second graders are not yet capable of seeing that a base-ten "long" is equivalent to ten unit cubes. In one second-grade classroom a group of teachers and I switched to mung beans as counters and ran a bead of glue down popsicle sticks. Ten mung beans fit nicely into the glue of each stick. We then glued together ten bean sticks, creating a "raft" worth one hundred beans. The students used the raft, the ten-bean sticks, and individual beans to work out operations and problems. To help students focus on the foundational constructs of our base-ten numeration system we might also introduce (not all at once) small plastic cups containing ten counter units, bundling sticks, ten frames, and rekenreks.

Model Development and Multiple Embodiments

The theoretical framework for model-development sequences is largely based on Dienes' theory of multiple embodiments. Dienes emphasized that students need to go beyond thinking *with* a given model (i.e., embodiment, or classroom mathematical manipulative) to also thinking *about* it. To do so, students need to encounter a concept represented in multiple embodiments (i.e., models) so that individuals will not solely attend to irrelevant features that are inevitably embedded in specific manipulatives. By using multiple embodiments to represent a concept, students begin to recognize the general, abstract concepts that the various embodiments are intended to convey. Similarly, by creating, adapting, and comparing several structurally similar embodiments of a mathematical model, students have opportunities to compare and contrast models, to think about the similarities and difference among them, and to investigate the relationships among alternative models. The generalizing of knowledge from the initial situation to an unfamiliar, yet somewhat close, situation is what constitutes *transfer* from a model and modeling perspective.

Cycles of Reconceptualization

Models are not usually physical objects. Models are ways that students conceive of conceptual systems, expressed in a variety of representations. The creation of a model is like examining an embodiment and can go through *cycles of reconceptualization*, analogous to investigating multiple embodiments.

Initially, students may be presented with a real-life situation, unstructured, messy, warts and all, referred to as a *model-eliciting activity*. A "good" problem is one that requires thought and discussion, eliciting students' interpretations of the situation described in the problem. Working in small groups of three, students share their insights about how to work on the problem. The goal of the activity is to "develop, test, revise and refine powerful, sharable, and re-usable conceptual tools that involve much more than simple answers to questions of the type emphasized in traditional textbooks and tests" (Lesh et al. 2003, 41).

Students *begin* their learning experience by solving real-life applied problems that require them to create, revise, or adapt a mathematical way of thinking (i.e., a mathematical model). Thus, if initial problems given to students are "model eliciting," students are expected to bring their own personal meaning to bear on a problem and to test and revise their interpretation as they grapple with the problem situation. "Students are assumed to simultaneously gain an increasing understanding of both the problem situation and their own mathematization of the problem over a series of modeling cycles" (Lesh and Zawojewski 2006, 54).

An Example of Modeling: Chocolate Algebra

The example of math modeling I describe here encourages the students to explore patterns of covariation with two variables in a T-table within a context of buying chocolate candy. Later they will use contexts of their own choosing. They go through the process of creating three different representations—tables, graphs, and equations—each of which requires a cycle of reconceptualization that in the debriefing is connected to other representations. These math-to-math connections make it possible for students to translate between representations easily and with full understanding.

Stephanie Krizmis teaches middle school math half-time while spending the other half as a math coach for the teachers in her building, the Prairie School in Schaumburg (Illinois) School District. She has been with me as a consultant to the Jenks, Oklahoma, schools, where we team-taught math activities through demonstration lessons in a variety of different classrooms.

We were given a classroom of thirty-six third graders and told that three of the students had aides with them. There was quite a mixture of abilities. We started with a little mental math of a hypothetical situation that was nonetheless quite imaginable for the students. "Your Uncle Art gave you $10 and asked you to go to the store and buy Tootsie Rolls and Hershey Bars. Tax included, a canister of Tootsie Rolls cost $1 and the big Hershey Bars cost $2." I held up a canister and a bar. "If you want to spend all of your $10 and have all chocolate, no change, what are all the ways you could do that?" Some kids raised their hands and some blurted out possibilities. We wrote down on the whiteboard what they said: 10 Tootsie Rolls, 4 Tootsie Rolls and 3 Hershey bars. We stopped them and asked, "Can we just abbreviate these ideas as [10 TR] and [4 TR & 3 HB]?" We paused and had them do a whole-class version of a KWC, which they had no trouble doing. They appeared to like the constraint of "all chocolate, no change." For the W, they agreed that we would look for all the ways to spend $10.

They gave us some more solutions: [5 HB] [2 TR & 4 HB] [1 HB & 8 TR]. "Are all these true solutions? Here is how to check and make sure." We gave each pair of students a packet of play money. It contained 15 $2 bills and 15 $1 bills. Why so much? We wanted them to use a $2 bill to represent a purchase of a Hershey Bar and a $1 bill to represent the purchase of a canister of Tootsie Rolls. Thereafter we suggested they use the play money, if they wanted to help their group check or find different ways. The play money served as a manipulative, representing the actual items.

We asked, "Did you figure out all the different things you could do?" They thought so but were not certain. "We made a recorded list of what you said, which is good, but let's organize it. How could we do that?" Working with partners, three at a table, they took out their small whiteboards and tried to construct a table. I suggested that we do it together. We put the Hershey Bar and a $2 bill into the lip of the whiteboard toward the left side and the canister of Tootsie Rolls and a $1 bill on the right side. Then Stephanie drew a large *T* on the whiteboard with the vertical part of the *T* separating the two items. She made column headings for the T-table: $2 HB on the left and $1 TR on the right. At the top right of the table we added "to be spent" and in this case "$10."

"What is the most HBs you could buy?" 5 was the resounding answer. Instead of writing it down immediately, I said, "Let's try 6." I varied the language a little and said, "If the HBs cost $2 *apiece*, how much would 6 of them cost?" $12 was their reply. "Can we do that?" "No!" "Why not?" "We only have $10!" they said in unison.

We had one more thing to add. I wrote down the 5 under the $2 HB column and said, "If HBs cost $2 apiece, how much would 5 of them cost?" "$10," they shouted. I drew a small square in the corner of the cell and inserted "$10." We had to complete the information for that row. I asked, "How much do you have left to spend on TRs?" "None" and "We spent it all on HBs" were their replies. Figure 4.1 shows what we created thus far.

To check their understanding, we asked them what the "5" in the table meant. They knew.

So we asked them what would come next. Most agreed that 4 HBs and 2 TRs would. We quickly rehearsed the same way of talking

$2 HB	$1 TR	to be spent	$10
$10	$0		
5	**0**		

Figure 4.1

about it as before: "4 HBs at $2 apiece would cost how much?" $8! We entered 4 in the next row and $8 in the little box in the corner. Now came a slight shift. "That will leave you with how much money to spend on TRs?" $2!

Then we entered $2 in the little box under the TRs. "Can we get that as change?" "No!" They shouted. "Can we buy 1 TR?" Some hesitated. "Not if we have to spend all of the $10," they said.

We asked them to complete the table by going down by the next number of HBs they could get. They all found the other ways. Most had been listed in the initial recording of possibilities. See Figure 4.2. We asked them how they knew that they had found all the ways and got the same response I have had in other classrooms many times before. "We tried all the ways." "How do you know you tried all the ways?" I was waiting for a response such as: "We systematically, in order, went through the possible HBs" or "I see a pattern." Often their response is: "We used the biggest number of HBs (5) and carefully went down by 1 until we got to 0." If no one mentions

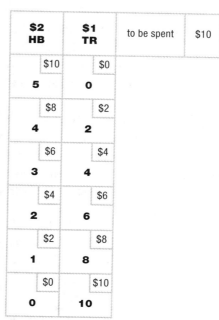

$2 HB	$1 TR	to be spent	$10
$10	$0		
5	**0**		
$8	$2		
4	**2**		
$6	$4		
3	**4**		
$4	$6		
2	**6**		
$2	$8		
1	**8**		
$0	$10		
0	**10**		

Figure 4.2

seeing a pattern, we go there next in the debriefing and say: "Look at the table. Do you see any patterns in these data?"

At that moment at Jenks Elementary School, a heated discussion erupted at a table in the corner. A frail-looking little girl was in a very agitated state. As I got closer she was explaining to her group several patterns that she saw. They could not follow her as she spoke rapidly and excitedly. She was getting frustrated with her group. I asked her to show me what she had seen. I was impressed. So I told her to wait and we'd ask her to explain her thinking to the class.

The students said, "One side goes down and the other goes up." We asked, "Why?" Some replied in virtual unison: "Because you always must spend $10, so if you buy less of one kind, you have to buy more of the other." Others said things like: "The number of Hershey Bars goes down by 1 and the number of Tootsie Rolls goes up by 2." "Does this always happen?" we asked. They said, "Yes!" Again we asked, "Why?" I told Stephanie to call on the excited little girl; she jumped up and ran over to the T-chart. She burst out with, "It is because of the money. Look at the little boxes in the corners. Every time we buy 1 less HB we save $2, but we have to spend it over on the other side, and that $2 can buy us 2 TRs. And another pattern is there in the money corners, too. The cost of the HBs goes down by the even numbers: $10, $8, $6, $4, $2, $0, and the same numbers are reversed in the cost of the TRs: $0, $2, $4, $6, $8, $10." She was beaming. We thanked her.

I had never attempted this activity with thirty-six students of such varied backgrounds. The objective was to introduce them to a T-table and to have them realize its value. We had taken forty minutes. So I released the students and planned to talk with the dozen teachers who'd been observing. But first, little Miss Patterns came running up to me and gave me a big hug and said, "I love you!" She went skipping off. That kept me going for another entire year.

Then her teacher came up to me and told me the girl's story. She always excelled at arithmetic and knew her math facts very well. Six months ago she had an epileptic seizure and had lost all memory of math facts. She is absolutely blank about multiplication facts. I was astonished and asked, "How could she do the task that we just did?" She replied, "She sees patterns everywhere!"

I include this activity here because it epitomizes the power of creating a mathematical model, initially realizing the patterns of covariation in a T-table and later the intricacies of the three powerfully connected representations: tables, graphs, and equations. If students in intermediate grades 3–5 were introduced to this model, they could build the prerequisite knowledge to tackle algebra in middle school.

Alice Valencia teaches a bilingual class of third graders at Twain Elementary School, in the Wheeling (Illinois) School District. She took her students further using the Hershey Bar and Tootsie Roll problem than Stephanie and I were able to take our students in the previous demonstration lesson. They experienced additional cycles.

I first asked my students, in pairs, to share the name of their favorite candy bar and how often they got to eat one. Then we talked about this as a whole class and found out it wasn't very often. Health concerns and parents' permission were the two main reasons for their limited consumption. We also talked about the price of different kinds of candy. Most of them did not know.

Then I presented the problem:

You have $10 to spend on Hershey's Chocolate Bars that cost $2 each and bags of Tootsie Rolls that cost $1 each. Find as many different combinations as you can of ways to spend your money. You have to spend all your money. There are no taxes.

We discussed the problem and collectively filled in a KWC organizer using think-pair-share. Most students had no trouble understanding the problem and expressing what they had to do.

I gave 12 fake $2 bills to each child, mentioning that bills in this denomination really exist but are not very common. (Some students had seen some real ones.) I also gave them each 15 fake $1 bills. I wanted them to have more of each than the number they were going to need.

Students started working independently. After they found their first answer, some students thought they were done. I referred them back to the question. A few were surprised there was going to be more than one correct answer. Finally children began claiming they had found all the combinations. I asked them to explain how they knew their individual combinations were correct. Explanations were very similar: "However I spend my money, it has to amount to $10." I also asked how they knew they had found the total number of possible combinations. This required a little more thinking.

"Well, I counted and I have 6 answers."

"That's right. But how do you know there are no more answers? Are you sure? Why?"

This question prompted them to organize their combinations. After a bit more thinking, they realized there could not be any more combinations because they had started at 0 chocolate bars and gone in order to arrive at 0 bags of Tootsie Rolls. "I have the ends and everything in between."

We shared our findings as a class. Children explained their work, displaying it on a document camera as they did so.

Next I handed out copies of a blank table they could use to organize the combinations. At the top of the left column, they wrote *HB* and *$2*. They headed the right column *TR* and *$1*. In a small box to the right of the columns, they wrote the total amount of money they had to spend, *$10*.

I had them start filling out the table by writing in the largest number of Hershey Bars we could buy. They wrote *5* in the top box of the right column and *$10* in the box-within-the-box. Then they filled in the corresponding amounts for the TR column: *0* and *$0.00*. They continued with each descending number of Hershey Bars and the corresponding increasing number of bags of Tootsie Rolls, as in Figure 4.3.

$2 HB	$1 TR	to be spent	$10
$10	$0		
5	0		
$8	$2		
4	2		
$6	$4		
3	4		
$4	$6		
2	6		
$2	$8		
1	8		
$0	$10		
0	10		

Figure 4.3

After they had filled in the table, we discussed why we would want to do it in order. Students eagerly shared their discovery: "So we can make sure we have all the answers." I prompted them to look for patterns in the table. After studying it, they noticed that the HB column went down by 1 and the TR column increased by 2. They did not notice any other pattern.

At the end of the period we talked about what they had learned: "Some problems have more than just one answer." "It is better when we start with all of one and none of the other." I asked if they thought they would always have all of one and none of the other. They answered, "If you have $10, you can have either 5 Hershey Bars or 10 Tootsie Rolls. And that is all of one and none of the other." One child talked about the strategy he used, changing one for the other to find the amounts. I left it at that.

At the beginning of the following class, we recapped what we had learned so far and went on to the second problem:

You have $27.00 to spend on M&Ms that cost $5.00 a bag and Tootsie Rolls that cost $1 a bag. Find as many combinations as you can of ways to spend your money. You have to spend all your money. There are no taxes.

Since the problem was very similar to the previous one, children immediately started making combinations of amounts totaling $27. When three-quarters of the students had finished, we began sharing answers. We created a table (Figure 4.4), and I asked what patterns they noticed. They noted that M&Ms column went down by 1 and the TR column went up by 5. I asked if they saw something else. One girl said that the dollar value by which the M&Ms decreased "crossed" (corresponded to) the dollar value by which the Tootsie Rolls increased. The children also realized that they could *not* have all of one and none of the other at the beginning and end of the table.

The next day we tried a third problem:

You have $40 to spend on Ring Pops that cost $5 a bag and Skittles that cost $2 a bag. Find as many combinations as you can of ways to spend your money. You have to spend all your money. There are no taxes.

Very soon I heard, "Wait, this is not working like the other two." I encouraged them to keep trying. After a bit more work, they discovered that 2 bags of Ring Pops were equal to 5 bags of Skittles. The children who started with the largest number of Ring Pops bags they could buy quickly arrived at the solution (see Figure 4.5).

$5 MM	$1 TR	to be spent	$27
$25 / 5	$2 / 2		
$20 / 4	$7 / 7		
$15 / 3	$12 / 12		
$10 / 2	$17 / 17		
$5 / 1	$22 / 22		
$0 / 0	$27 / 27		

Figure 4.4

$5 RP	$2 SK	to be spent	$40
$40 / 8	$0 / 0		
$30 / 6	$10 / 5		
$20 / 4	$20 / 10		
$10 / 2	$30 / 15		
$0 / 0	$40 / 20		

Figure 4.5

We shared our answers, realizing that this time we could again have none of either item. We noticed the down-by-two-up-by-five pattern. This time more children mentioned the dollar-value crossover; two children even said they had used this fact to arrive at the solution. I was on cloud nine.

The first time I did this activity was as a demonstration lesson with third graders for a highly skeptical group of teachers many years ago. The eighteen students were wonderfully well behaved (probably because there were six teachers in the back of the classroom). No one in the room had peanut allergies, and the hope of chocolate was in the air. They sailed through the activities and all the patterns of the three tables (Figures 4.3, 4.4, and 4.5) in an hour. My objective was modest: that they would understand how a T-table worked, never having seen one before that day. As I was wrapping up, one of the children asked me if they could do some of these tables for homework.

I looked at the teacher whose eyes were wide open, as was her mouth. She nodded her approval. Then other kids chimed in, "Can we buy all 3 candies?" We negotiated with them, and they went to recess with a small bag of M&Ms, promising to return tomorrow with ways to buy all 3 items, $5, $2, and $1, and to spend all $99. The pages of arithmetic practiced that night was ten times what any teacher would have assigned!

The next time I tried this activity in a fourth-grade classroom, and these students also found many patterns in the tables. For homework I suggested they create their own problem for the class to solve. It would have two items at different prices, a total amount of money required to be spent, and multiple possible answers. The most entrepreneurial child was a young lady who desired Persian vases at $4,000 apiece, Persian rugs at $10,000 apiece, and she had a million dollars to spend. She had found many answers!

Extensions: Chocolate Algebra

As the years unfolded, I continued trying different versions of the activity and using more class time. Fourth and fifth graders were asked to create a graph for each table. The links between table and graph and the items they represented became very clear to students. The numbers in the columns of the table became the values of two variables, x and y. Each row in the table became a point on the coordinate graph, a solution to the problem of finding all the ways of spending all the money. Each solution point could be represented by (x, y). For example, from the table in Figure 4.5, students could be certain that points must lie in the first quadrant where all values were positive, because they referred to real items [i.e., (8,0); (6,5); (4,10); (2,15) and (0,20)]. And for special surprise, these points all were in a straight line, extending from high on the vertical axis down to hit the horizontal axis. See the graph in Figure 4.6.

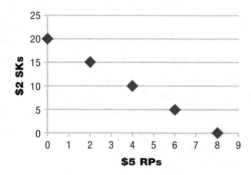

Figure 4.6

The points (8,0) and (0,20) have a particular meaning in this context—all of one kind of candy and none of the other. If you start at the x-intercept (8,0) and go down 2 (to the left) and up 5 on the y-scale, you'd be at point (6,5), giving additional meaning to the pattern of down by 2 (–2) and up by 5 (+5) that the students found in the table. All consecutive points can be found that way.

The students frequently ask about the line that they'd like to draw through the solution points. We ask them questions such as: "What would a solid line segment from (8,0) to (0,20) mean to you?" A solid line would mean that there would be a great many solutions to the original question. But there are only 5 solutions that make sense. You can't buy part of a candy bar. These 5 are the only solutions because a major *constraint* is that you must buy a whole number of items of each kind (technically, we'd call them *positive integers*). We could put in a *dashed line* that would indicate no solutions between the 5 points.

From Concrete to Abstract: The Meaning of Slope

The students also ask about the "tilt" of the line. They have only seen lines that start in the *origin* and go up on both axes. We ask the students to think about these two candies while we play a little "what if" game. What would a graph of points look like if I gave you a credit card and said you could spend as much money as you want to but you must always buy the same number of each candy? That question always gets them imagining. "We have points going up from (1,1), (2,2) . . . (100, 100)!" This is a very different situation. If one variable goes up, the other must also. We call these *positive slope* situations. But when you are constrained by the situation to spend a specific amount of money, then when one variable goes up, the other one must go down. We call these *negative slope* situations.

The slope of a line can be thought of in various ways: how "steep" the slope is, like the slope of a mountain. It can be the rate of change of one variable compared to the change in the other variable. We talked about the pattern in the table as down by 2 and up by 5. We measure the slope as the change in the y variable compared to the change in the x variable or a +5/–2 *ratio*. We can look at the slope in a number of situations and their tables. For example, students need to see that being given a specific amount more money to spend will not affect the slope, because the pattern in the table remains the same. The solutions are different, but the points line up in parallel lines to one another.

For some fifth- and sixth-grade classes, we have continued the exploration with yet another set of representations. We go back to the original table and add another row at the bottom. See Figure 4.7. We put an x in the table stating that, "What if I bought x number of the RP candy? How much would they cost?" "How would I know what to put in the box in the corner?" They recall that they merely had to multiply $5 times the number of RPs bought: $5x or simply 5x. We repeated these questions for the y variable (SK). Then the teacher or I would write on the whiteboard, "The cost of the RPs plus the cost of the SKs equals the money to be spent."

From this statement, we can write the standard equation, $5x + 2y = 40$. Every symbol and sign has a specific meaning in the students' minds. They know what each refers to. If the students are in algebra at the time, we might go a little further and rearrange the terms to isolate y

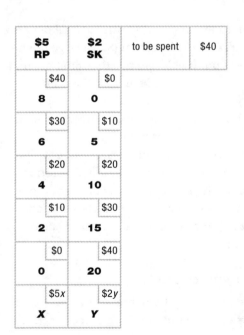

Figure 4.7

to get the y-intercept form of the equation $y = -(5/2)x + 20$. The 20 signifies that when $x = 0$, we are left with 20 for our value of y that is the y-intercept.

In the young minds of our students, the three representations of table, graph, and equation are explicitly braided together, each revealing something different about the real situation. Older students, whose sense of the relationship among the three representations was based on a textbook giving them an equation and telling them to make a table of values with at least three points and then graph the values in the table, often react to this activity with, "This makes so such more sense than the way the book does it" and "Why didn't you show this to us first?"

If you find these activities intriguing, you can read in my previous book *Understanding Middle School Math* (Hyde et al. 2009) how sixth-grade teacher Susan Friedlander took her students through multiple cycles of reconceptualization. In that book, she also describes a room renovation problem patterned after Lesh's carpentry problem. A different example of a model-building activity may be seen on pages 142–150 in my book *Comprehending Math* (2006).

In the next chapter, I will describe in some details the specific things that I do and say in helping students become problem solvers and creators of math models. The methods that I use require that you consciously combine mathematical concepts with cognitive principles and appropriate language. When these three are woven together into a metaphorical braid, they become mutually supportive. If any of the three braided elements is ignored or severed, the braid collapses.

CHAPTER

5

Exploring the Braid Model of Problem Solving

THE BRAID MODEL OF PROBLEM SOLVING is a flexible method of solving mathematical problems using adaptations of reading comprehension strategies, especially in the initial understanding phase of working on a math problem. It provides a structure for students to productively think about the mathematics they could use. The Braid Model takes advantage of the cognitive processes on which both reading/language arts and mathematics depend.

The Origins of the Braid Model

The ideas underlying the Braid Model go back to my work with reading and language arts colleagues, especially Marilyn Bizar, with whom I wrote *Thinking in Context: Teaching Cognitive Processes Across the Elementary School Curriculum* (1989). As we realized the common aspects of cognition prevalent in our disciplines, our collaboration intensified. With Smokey Daniels and Steve Zemelman, we began the Best Practice network in 1991 in the Chicago Public Schools using thirty-hour school-based workshops in which teachers were introduced to and experienced the practices we promoted in reading, writing, and mathematics.

The Development of the Teaching for Conceptual Integration Program

In 2004 with the help of half a dozen colleagues, I created a program called Teaching for Conceptual Integration (TCI). Designed to serve self-contained elementary school teachers who taught multiple subjects to their students, the program had its roots in the Best Practice network and conceptual integration theory, also known as *blend theory*, from cognitive science. Anne Reichel was my partner in this venture.

Cognitive researchers were finding social phenomena that were explained by blend theory on a regular basis. Linguists and other language-oriented professionals were using blend theory to examine the power of figurative language. Mathematicians were finding conceptual metaphors that were layered on top of one another to create that wonderfully coherent body of knowledge. We drew heavily upon the work of Lakoff and Nuñez (2000), Fauconnier and Turner (2002), and a dozen articles written by other cognitive scientists to help us think deeply about how to apply their theoretical notions to the integration of subject areas.

We started with several assumptions that were consistent with blend theory:

1. Each area would have parts that were not integrated; some parts would stand alone.
2. We would have to understand how to integrate two areas before attempting to integrate more than two.
3. When a new entity emerged from the blending, the contribution of each area should be recognizable.

As we planned the program, we knew we were also creating curriculum for the schools that the teachers in the program could use. We came to realize that there were three main things that could be integrated:

1. concepts (e.g., density explained in science as the packing together of molecules, in mathematics as mass per unit volume, and in social studies as population relative to area)
2. cognitive processes (e.g., making connections among concepts)
3. teaching methods (e.g., small-group collaboration).

First, we identified concepts that used the same concept label in different subject areas. The experts in the subject on the design team drew from the best books and articles to design the subject matter and delineate for the team what they had found. Of special note were the publications from subject matter professional organizations that arranged the scope and sequence of their area. Next, we looked at the processes of thinking used in that subject area to build understanding of concepts. What is inquiry in each area? How is new knowledge generated? Finally, we identified what teachers did to help students learn the characteristic thinking in each subject area.

We took the four main subject areas of the curriculum and created six pairings of "dual" courses:

1. Integrated Reading / Language Arts and Mathematics
2. Integrated Reading / Language Arts and Social Studies
3. Integrated Reading / Language Arts and Science
4. Integrated Mathematics and Science
5. Integrated Mathematics and Social Studies
6. Integrated Science and Social Studies

These became six "dual" courses in a master's degree program in curriculum and instruction. Other courses included Curriculum Theory, Instructional Practices, Cognition and Instruction, Educational Research, and Educational History and Philosophy. These five more general courses allowed our faculty to go after big ideas that cut across all subject areas, while the dual courses allowed us to focus on what can be successfully integrated and what needs to be kept separate.

I directed the TCI program and taught the Cognition and Instruction course. Each of the paired subject area courses were team-taught by two professors (i.e., I taught the three courses that involved mathematics and teamed with three other people). I wrote *Comprehending Math* (2006) after teaching the course Integrating Reading / Language Arts and Mathematics, and the book has been the main text used in the course, which is now part of the master's degree program in mathematics education. That book was the first time I wrote about the Braid Model for problem solving, but obviously I had been exploring what could be meant by "integration of different school subject areas" for decades.

Why Call It the Braid Model?

Conceptual integration theory recognizes metaphorical thinking as especially powerful in conveying information. Therefore, I sought to find an apt metaphor to not only describe the information but also to give us new insights into relevant phenomena. I knew a little bit about braid theory and the related knot theory in topology from Martin Gardner's columns in *Scientific American*. The more I explored braid theory, the more excited I became.

I was fascinated by the Borromean rings—three rings connected in such a way that they were held together by virtue of their relationship to each other, not because they were locked together. If any one of the rings were severed, the other two rings would fall apart because no two rings were locked together. See Figure 5.1. I thought that was an excellent way to describe the relationship of mathematics, language, and cognition. When all three are present and consciously addressed by the teacher and students, understanding can flourish. Remove any one of the three and the other two cease to be as effective. Of course, the right kind of cognitive process, appropriate language, and good mathematical thinking must be used to keep the proper balance.

An Example of Our Analyses

Figure 5.1

Reading is a dynamic process of deriving meaning from written language. Readers interact with texts. They do not passively receive meaning; they create it for themselves. They draw on their prior knowledge to make sense of the content of the text. Impressed with the work of reading/language arts professors and teachers, reading specialists, children's authors, and school writers in-residence, we asked whether these theories and practices might be applied to math instruction.

1. Are students expected to construct their own meaning in mathematics?
2. Are students encouraged to own their problem solving—use mathematics for purposes they set for themselves?
3. Are students encouraged to problem solve for authentic purposes?
4. Are students encouraged to use mathematics voluntarily because they enjoy it or want to acquire information or fulfill personal goals?
5. How is mathematics instruction scaffolded?
6. Does the school help teachers and students build a rich, mathematically literate environment or community?
7. Are students encouraged to see the big picture, important concepts, vital connections versus isolated pieces of mathematics?
8. Is making mistakes seen as a natural part of learning mathematics? Is mathematics seen as a dynamic process that incorporates planning, drafting, revising, editing, and publishing?

Trying to answer these questions will give you an informative look at the culture of mathematics teaching in this country and may raise more questions in your mind. Think just about question 1. Do we see learning math as meaning making? Or do we see it as transmitted by the teacher to the students? Von Glasersfeld states:

The assumption that conceptual structures could be carried from teachers (or books) to students by means of language or other representational media is an integral part of the traditional theory of teaching. Constructivism, however, has emphasized that this is a fallacy. Words, diagrams, pictures, and, I would add, mathematical formulae, do not contain meanings; they can only elicit them from a repertoire that is already present in the listener or reader. (2003, 3)

And thinking about questions 2–4 leads us to ask: How much would we have to stretch to offer our students a math curriculum that included ownership, authentic purposes, and voluntary math for personal goals? How would we begin to define such terms, let alone reach consensus on their meaning?

Question 5 leads to the further questions: What might scaffolding look like in mathematics? A scaffold does not do the work for a painter or plasterer; it stands alongside the building as a means to do the work. Scaffolding is not providing hints or showing students how to get started. It is a way of making the problem accessible, perhaps asking a question that focuses attention on something students have overlooked.

Thinking about question 6: What would a rich, mathematically literate environment look like? What artifacts would we see? These are some: games, puzzles, and manipulatives (recreational mathematics is not an oxymoron); student math work of all kinds (in two and three dimensions) displayed on the walls and hung from the ceiling; colors and shapes that would fool one into thinking they were in an art room.

For many years, NCTM has exhorted teachers to help students see mathematics as a coherent whole, as suggested in question 7, rather than as factoids plastered on a wall. But we ourselves have been taught in a fragmented way. As learners, how many of us experienced the interconnectedness of concepts and relationships among ideas in mathematics? I certainly didn't. I am still realizing connections among mathematical concepts that were "taught" to me in separate boxes.

And finally, question 8. Do we lead students to believe that there is only one right answer and getting it quickly is our major goal? Are accuracy, speed, and precision the only virtues we value? If we didn't expect students to make mistakes, why did we give them pencils and erasers? Everyone makes mistakes, but what do they learn from them?

A Matrix Analysis

To my knowledge no one has attempted to integrate reading and mathematics as thoroughly as we did in TCI. No one has conceived of mathematical problem solving as we have. No one has systematically examined the relationships among reading/language arts, mathematical problem solving, and cognitive processes as we have.

To begin with, we created a matrix in which seven reading comprehension strategies (Keene and Zimmermann 2007; Harvey and Goudvis 2007) intersected with the five math processes of NCTM 2000 (see Figure 5.2). For each cell we asked, "What principles from cognitive psychology can we use to modify this reading strategy in a way that will help students do this math process?" This question is at the heart of the integration because it addresses all three components of the braid. It is not merely asking us to integrate reading and math in any way we might choose. It asks us to formulate our questions to carefully consider new possibilities from a cognitive perspective. For example, for the cell in row 2, column 1, we asked, "What kinds of metacognitive self-questioning can students use to enhance their problem solving?" After experimentation, we created a math KWC (an adaptation of the KWL in Blachowicz and Ogle 2001):

- What do I Know for sure?
- What do I Want to find out?
- Are there any special Conditions?

Reading Comprehension Strategies	Mathematical Processes				
	Problem Solving	Reasoning and Proof	Connections	Communication	Representation
Making connections					
Asking questions					
Visualizing					
Inferring					
Predicting					
Determining importance					
Synthesizing					

Figure 5.2

Our KWC questions provide structure and focus for students while they read a story problem. The teacher models these questions for the whole class, and the students raise these same questions when they discuss the problem in small groups or work on the problem individually.

Row 1, column 5 might suggest that we directly model how we make connections among representations. This is called "translating between representations." From a cognitive perspective, representations can be expressions of the mental model the student has in mind. We also see the value of creating representations as a critically important aspect of problem-solving strategies described in the previous chapter.

The Braid Model

After trying our adapted comprehension strategies with a variety of math problems (traditional story problems, open-ended or extended-response problems, mathematical modeling tasks), we created the Braid Model of problem solving, shown in Figure 5.3.

At first glance, this may look like much too much to do. Like anything that is important in teaching, it takes a little time and practice to make it work. When the Braid Model does work, it flows easily. Therefore, let's examine this approach one step at a time.

Understanding the Problem

The process of understanding the problem is very fluid, not lockstep. Model it by talking through your thoughts out loud. Prompt students to think about aspects of the problem by asking questions that will help them clarify their thinking. The Braid Model encourages students to think about the problem in a variety of ways.

Visualizing. Model what the students should be doing by asking the questions out loud. Students have to read the entire description of the situation, not take shortcuts like looking for the key words. Do they see images or picture in their minds? Can they imagine the situation? Have them form a mental image of one piece of the problem at a time, sentence by sentence (project the problem or display it on a poster or flip chart; for young children, you can present the problem orally). Some children do not form mental images as they read, but with prompting they can develop this important habit.

Asking questions. KWC is a great metacognitive prompt, because it provides a structure for discussion. The K question elicits information. W is the task definition. C is a place for (1) things students are uncertain about; (2) obvious things that are

Understanding the Problem/Reading the Story

Visualizing

Do I see pictures in my mind?

How do they help me understand the situation?

Imagine the situation. What is going on here?

Asking questions/discussing the problem in small groups

K: What do I know for sure?

W: What do I want to figure out, find out, or do?

C: Are there any special conditions, rules, or tricks I have to watch out for?

Making connections

Math-to-self:

What does this situation remind me of?

Have I ever been in any situation like this?

Math-to-world:

Is this related to things I've seen in social studies, science, the arts, or anywhere?

Math-to-math:

What main mathematical idea is happening here?

Where have I seen this idea before?

What other math ideas are related to this one?

Can I use them to help me with this problem?

Inferring

What inferences have I made? For each connection, what is its significance?

When I look back at my *K* and *C* notes, which are facts and which are inferences?

Are my inferences accurate?

Planning How to Solve the Problem

What **representations** can I use to help me solve the problem? Which problem-solving **strategy** will help me the most in this situation?

Make a model	Draw a picture	Make an organized list
Act it out	Make a table	Write an equation
Find a pattern	Use logical reasoning	Draw a diagram
Work backward	Solve a simpler problem	Predict and test

Carrying out the plan/solving the problem

Work on the problem using a **strategy**.

Does this strategy show me something I didn't see before now?

Should I try another strategy?

Am I able to **infer** any **patterns**?

Am I able to **predict** based on this inferred pattern?

Looking back/checking

Does my answer make sense for the problem?

Is there a **pattern** that makes the answer reasonable?

What **connections** link this problem and answer to the big ideas of mathematics I am learning? Is there another way to do this? Have I made an **assumption**?

Figure 5.3

not literally stated but need to be acknowledged; and (3) constraints on the problem or its solution (for example, purchasing more wallpaper than the square footage necessary to cover the walls in order to accommodate matching a pattern, as well as allow for mistakes). Occasionally students will not realize all the things that could be under C until they begin to create representations of the problem; don't prompt them to find every special condition *you* can think of. In the end, it doesn't matter whether an important piece of information is put in the K or C category, only that it is included.

With younger children you might ask the following questions orally:

- What do you think about that/it?
- What can you tell me about this situation?
- What do you know about it already?
- What do you think will happen?
- Is there anything weird or strange about this?
- Does anything surprise you?

One might be tempted to say that gifted math students don't need the KWC structure. However, they do need to be able to articulate their thinking. And KWC is a comfortable way for anxious or struggling math students to get started. For all students, thinking about the C is a second chance to rethink what they think they know. (Some teachers combine KWC with visualization, K being what students visualize and C being what they are not sure is true.)

Making connections. Math-to-self connections are fairly easy. Math-to-world connections are principally those to science and social studies. The most difficult connections are math-to-math. Students often use sticky notes to record connections when reading, but a math story problem is often only a paragraph long. Students can either highlight or underline the three kinds of connections in different colors. They could also jot down their responses on a graphic organizer.

Inferring. Students pull many pieces of information together in their attempt to understand the problem. Inferences are natural and acceptable (we all make them, all the time), but it is prudent to realize when you are drawing a inference rather than stating a fact. Students need to make sure they have thought through the problem and check that their inferences are accurate. On the other hand, they may not fully appreciate all the conceptual possibilities until they experience them, and you don't want to force them into a particular interpretation. Therefore, they may be better off plowing ahead.

Planning How to Solve the Problem

Once students understand the problem, the next step is to use various strategies to think through how to reach a solution. This planning step should not be obsessive or cause friction in the group. Students just need enough time to pause and think about what they ought to do next.

Carrying Out the Plan/Solving the Problem

While the Braid Model asks students to use representational strategies to decide how to solve a problem, it is even more concerned with metacognition. Students should ask themselves whether a strategy is showing them something they hadn't realized before working with it. If the strategy doesn't appear to be productive, they should try a different one. It is also a good time to remind them to try to discern a pattern.

Looking Back/Checking

I have yet to meet a student who loved to check his or her work! It's a habit students need to develop. When the problem has been solved, students believe they are done; off come their thinking caps. Not quite. The problem-solving process needs to be debriefed. You take the lead here by asking questions about:

1. the solutions they found based on their interpretation of the task
2. the strategies they used
3. the patterns they discerned
4. the math concepts they used.

You will know what questions to ask because you will have listened to the students talk about their work. This is the time for you to explain the key concepts in the activity. Your explanations can be directly related to the conceptions they have expressed. These explanations may be quite different from the general, deductive explanation given in a textbook, and there is a much better chance that the students will connect with and remember them.

To make sense of a solution or to determine if it is reasonable, students need to look back at the original problem and their KWC notes. They can also determine whether there is a connection to a big idea in mathematics. A problem is worth spending time on because it develops students' understanding of an important concept. When you debrief students, your goal is for them to see patterns or concepts and how they are related to the big ideas that have surfaced.

Loretta Johnson and Laura Meehan are instructional coaches in the Barrington (Illinois) school district. They are very concerned with the kinds of connections their challenging bunch of third graders were making. They chose to experiment with the Braid Model to see if they could flexibly adapt it to integrate math, science, and reading, all with a cognitive perspective. Could they use a science text to develop a real-life context for math problem solving in which the students would suggest the questions for mathematical inquiry?

Students at all grade levels struggle to apply math and reading strategies across the content areas. During students' formative years, we guide them to use reading and math strategies but tend to do so in isolation. We avoid explicitly teaching the connections between reading and math. Without our guidance, students can't see the impact that reading strategies can have on problem solving. They see word problems as an out-of-context experience, as "school math." They hurriedly look for numbers and key words and apply a random operation to get a solution. They often fail to notice a series of steps: Once they have one part of an answer, they think their solution is complete. They miss the opportunity to understand math in the context of science and social studies—use number sense to comprehend the impact of the numbers.

Third graders learning about the solar system may read an article about the planets and find that Mercury travels around the sun so quickly that its year is only eighty-eight Earth days. Some of them may put an exclamation point next to this fact because it sounds exciting, but most nine-year-olds don't understand the concept of a year's being a different length on different planets because of the speed at which the planets travel. In order to help students truly understand this math content within their science lesson, we need to teach them to use reading strategies. During classroom discussion, we need to help students identify their ideas about Earth's rotation around the sun, visualize the situation, determine information that is relevant, infer the connection between planets in the same solar system, and synthesize how their own thinking about the topic has evolved as they have learned new information. If we can teach students to apply these reading strategies to mathematical information in other content areas, they will have a deeper connection with the content. When students own this process, they can retain and apply the information in new situations.

You may think you need to create new resources or purchase new materials in order to help your students synthesize content. However, you can create real-life, authentic contexts in math using your current science and social studies materials. We did.

We were teaching a third-grade advanced math class at Sunny Hill Elementary School, in Carpentersville, Illinois, in the spring of 2013. Seventy-six percent of the students at Sunny

Hill are Hispanic. Last year, 91 percent of the students received a free or reduced-price breakfast and lunch. The school has had mobility rates as high as 16 percent. More than half of the students have parents who do not speak English. This class comprised four girls and three boys pulled from four different classrooms (two of the classrooms had monolingual English instruction; the other two were bilingual one-way immersion classes taught primarily in Spanish). All the students had a strong number sense. We wondered whether these students could learn math in a real-life context, and we wanted to see whether they could apply reading strategies to other curricular areas.

To present a science unit about the solar system, we selected a chapter from a grade-level-appropriate book to support their understanding of the unit's essential questions. We looked at the Illinois Standards and Assessment Framework for Science and the Common Core State Standards for Mathematics and talked to their teachers to ensure that the students had the prerequisite knowledge in math to understand the information in the e-book.

We launched our lesson with a quick-write about the solar system in which students told us what they already knew about the solar system as a whole and the planets within it. Because the class was so small, after the quick-write we paired students and asked them to share their background knowledge with their partner. We listened to these conversations and then asked students to document their knowledge on a whole-class KWC chart. In effect, we were doing the K and the W more in the spirit of reading's KWL. We modified the chart because we knew that the C could be where we'd have the students identify inferences along with other special conditions. We wanted them to focus on inferences.

Next, each student, independently, read and annotated the selected chapter. We reminded them to use the symbols they used in reading workshop to mark the text, such as a question mark for questions or an exclamation point for new or interesting facts. We also asked them to use a new symbol, *I*, to note information that caused them to make an inference. We reviewed the definition of *inference* in student-friendly language.

After the students had read and annotated the text, we asked them to share their thoughts and notations with their partners and to fill in an individual KWC chart: facts they knew for sure from reading the text; questions they had that could be answered mathematically; special conditions; and inferences. We then charted this information as a class to create a cohesive list of their thoughts.

The students had great questions about the text, but they were not always mathematical. For example, one question was, "From where does Venus get the poisonous gases?" We challenged their thinking by asking, "Is that question something that you could answer using math?" They also asked questions with answers that didn't require problem solving ("How hot is the first planet closest to the sun?" and "How long has the solar system been around?" for example). We encouraged the students to go back and look for questions that could be answered using math. We then documented all their final questions. See Figure 5.4.

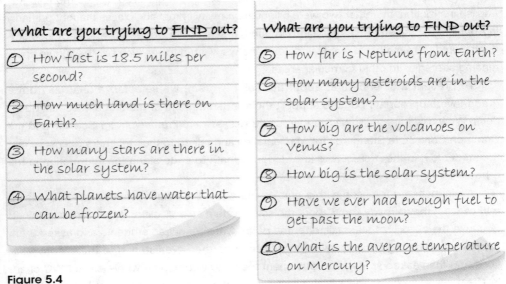

What are you trying to FIND out?

① How fast is 18.5 miles per second?

② How much land is there on Earth?

③ How many stars are there in the solar system?

④ What planets have water that can be frozen?

What are you trying to FIND out?

⑤ How far is Neptune from Earth?

⑥ How many asteroids are in the solar system?

⑦ How big are the volcanoes on Venus?

⑧ How big is the solar system?

⑨ Have we ever had enough fuel to get past the moon?

⑩ What is the average temperature on Mercury?

Figure 5.4

When we began discussing inferences, we found the students were having difficulty (perhaps because struggling with the English language affected their comprehension). Therefore, we came up with an inference as a group. The text revealed that the temperature on Mercury was about 800 degrees Fahrenheit and that the planet does not support animal or plant life. Students understood the magnitude of that temperature relative to the average temperatures we experience on Earth. They also were familiar with the water cycle. We discussed the impact such a high temperature would have on life and water, and they inferred that because the temperature is so high Mercury must not have water to sustain life.

At this point, we ran out of time. As we reflected on this first day, we were concerned about the students' questions. Many of them were exciting and advanced, but we didn't have the time necessary to develop the related concepts. Others were very abstract, like the number of stars in the galaxy. And we didn't have the time or space to model a distance of 18.5 miles or how far a human could travel in a second to give them a frame of reference. We decided that in the next session we would focus on the information about Mercury. The section about Mercury in the text was dense with information and data. These questions allowed us to work within the confines of time and space in the classroom.

At the start of day 2, we reviewed our KWC chart and the questions the students had written during our first session. We told them that we had decided to focus on information about Mercury and asked them to refer back to the section in the chapter about this planet. As a class, we wrote two more questions about Mercury that the students could answer using mathematical problem-solving skills. The three Mercury questions were:

- What is the average temperature on Mercury?

- How many hours does it take for Mercury to orbit the sun?

- How many degrees hotter is it during the day than at night on Mercury?

Each pair or trio then chose a question to answer. At this point, the students had no trouble applying their math knowledge to solving each problem. They had the prerequisite math skills to find a solution, and they were able to visually represent the steps. However, two of the teams didn't realize they had an error in their work.

Loretta visited the team that answered "How many hours does it take for Mercury to orbit the sun?" They had solved the problem in terms of minutes instead of hours. Instead of pointing out the error, Loretta asked them to label their work to create a context for the solution. In doing so, she had them reread their question to remind them of their intentions. They recognized that they had used the wrong unit of time and easily converted their solution (see Figure 5.5).

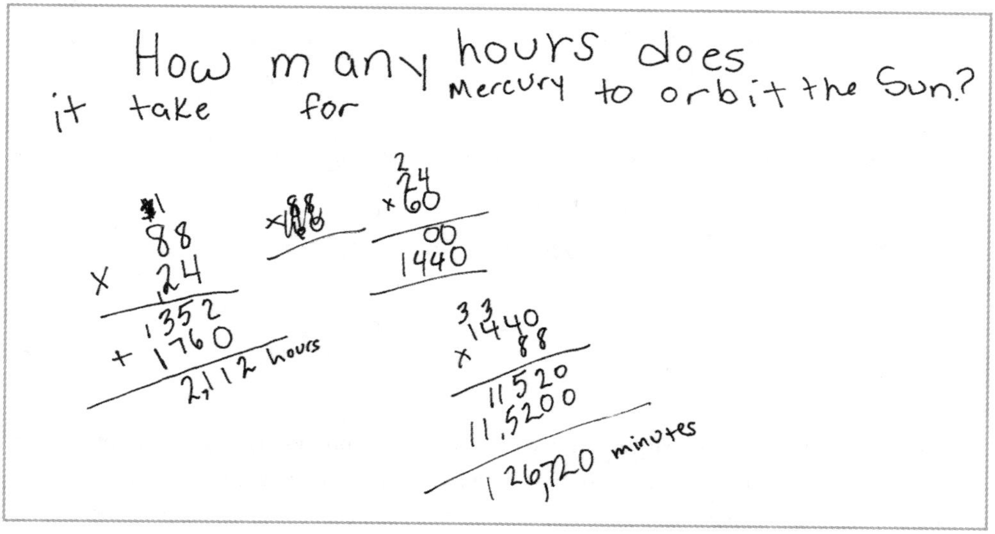

Figure 5.5

Laura visited the team that solved "How many degrees hotter does it get during the day than at night?" They had found the difference between the two temperature extremes on Mercury. However, they had considered the lower number, –297 degrees, to be a positive integer, and they found the difference between 870 degrees and 297 degrees. To help these students see the relative position of the two temperature readings, Laura had them draw a number line and label the distance of each number from zero. Once the students saw the relative position of the numbers, they saw that they needed to find the distance between the two numbers. By developing the context of the problem, the students were able to identify the correct steps as well as understand the wide range of temperatures on Mercury's surface (see Figure 5.6).

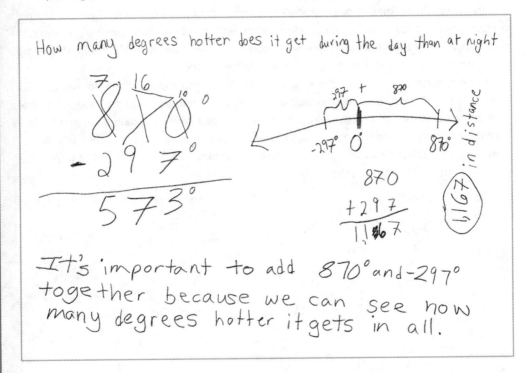

Figure 5.6

Reflecting on our work with these third graders, we identified some unexpected influences on learning. The students were self-conscious about this new learning experience. They were cautious about participating, perhaps because they were afraid of being wrong. Their apprehension seemed to hinder their curiosity. We were also surprised that they struggled to make inferences from the text. We expected advanced students to be comfortable using this reading strategy. The students had ideas for questions but didn't always know how to phrase the questions in a way that made sense to them and to us—perhaps because they weren't often asked to use the essential reading strategy of questioning in a math context. Students are used to being asked math questions but not to generating questions about math themselves. (This can be a challenge even for teachers!)

Our goal of integrating reading and math into other content areas will take time and effort. Our ultimate goal is for math strategies and reading strategies to partner, balance, and overlap. When this is done successfully, students will be able to create a context in their mind, which will lead to deeper comprehension.

The activity that Loretta and Laura conducted with these third graders shows the value as well as the difficulty of integrating math and science. They drew upon the spirit of the KWL from reading comprehension to deal with the factual content of science. Then they let the students generate questions that could be answered using mathematics. Either the students had difficulty in recognizing potential math problems within a science context or they became highly interested in the science facts. An important part of the Braid Model is realizing when the language used is literal or inferential. Loretta and Laura wisely adapted the model to make distinctions among ideas expressed under the C by coding inferences as I.

CHAPTER

6

Planning for and Implementing the Braid Model

I have found that when we recall the qualities and characteristics associated with the intellectual experiences we (or our students) have had, we can extract something more lasting than a recollection of the challenge itself. We can examine what happens in our minds and in our lives in new settings or learning contexts, when we are in the process of understanding. And what we can define and describe, we can increase, both in frequency and quality.

—Ellin Keene (2008)

THE PRECEDING CHAPTERS DESCRIBE a wide variety of things you might do to help your students understand mathematical concepts and solve math problems. They do not represent cut-and-dried steps or prescriptions. I have not created a program to be followed slavishly. Teaching is a dynamic, interactive activity. It does not lend itself to planning a highly structured sequence of moves by the teacher.

Conversely, many teachers have the idea that planning merely consists of listing the math topic to be addressed, the chapter in the text to be read and covered, all clearly written in their plan book so that the principal can read them. That is not what I consider planning to be.

Planning has always been an opportunity for me to *immerse* myself in the various possibilities for content and processes. I want to *rethink* the topic from every perspective I can imagine. Doing this has very frequently given me new insights into possible connections not found in traditional texts. For elementary school teachers whose favorite subject to teach is anything other than math, this kind of rethinking is essential if they are to develop understanding in their students. Teachers who experienced only the procedural, algorithmic math in school need to see conceptual alternatives.

Therefore, I have developed a set of "considerations" to ensure I have thoroughly thought about the aspects of the teaching and learning that I hope will occur. I have worded them in the form of questions intentionally. You are the best person to answer these questions and to determine what to adapt or modify to fit your classroom circumstances and the particular students you have.

Questions to Guide a Different Kind of Planning

When I, a young white man, began teaching in an all-black school, I had a lot to learn about and from my students. It would not be an exaggeration to say I was dabbling in cultural anthropology. I did not know what would work. I started keeping track of the activities I had tried, the questions I had asked, and how the students had responded. From this beginning, came a short list of *considerations*, questions I asked myself as I planned activities (see Figure 6.1). I taped the list on the wall above the desk where I planned each night for the next day.

1. What is the *concept* I want the students to understand? Is there a sequence of understandings they need to have?

2. What *mathematical thinking or cognitive process* do I want students to use?

3. What *prior experiences or conceptual understandings* are needed? Do the students have them? How can I build on these experiences and understandings?

4. In what *real-life situations* might students encounter or apply this concept?

5. What *questions* can I ask to intrigue students and initiate problem solving?

6. What *representations* could students create? What *manipulatives or physical materials* can help them see what is going on? What symbols must they understand?

7. What *patterns* (visual, spatial, or numerical) do I want students to see? What questions do I ask to help them see these patterns?

8. What *connections* are important for students to make? What questions do I ask to help them make these connections? What will help them connect the procedures to their understanding of the concept?

Figure 6.1

My first step was to deal directly with the *concept* I wanted my students to understand and immediately thereafter the *cognitive process* (mathematical thinking) they would use to grasp that concept. By distinguishing between content objectives and process objectives and addressing both, I avoided slipping into a routine of telling the students the procedural steps to follow and highlighting memorization.

As I planned activities I realized that some of these questions were sometimes irrelevant for the specific content we were investigating. On other occasions, they provoked me to go deeper into the mathematics. In those first few years of teaching, I thoroughly thought through each activity and wrote out key questions that I should ask the students at various times. I wouldn't say that I scripted the activity, but my list of follow-up questions prepared me for a range of student responses.

Although I am identifying the most important aspects of my own teaching, I am also concerned with maintaining good lesson "flow." The planning questions only help me determine what to include; the Braid Model suggests the sequence of these actions that should happen.

Before I present an example of planning, I'll share the more complex and comprehensive version of these considerations I have been using for the past fifteen years (see Figure 6.2). Although the list is longer and there are some additional considerations, on the whole I have simply expanded the original list to include nuances. Teachers have told me that they have benefited from trying out their planning with the shorter list and then making the transition to the longer list in a few weeks.

Considerations in Planning Mathematical Activities

1. **Big Ideas, Enduring Understandings, and Essential Concepts**

   What concept do I want the students to understand?
   To what prior knowledge should we as a class try to connect?
   Are there different "models" of the concept?
   Should I break down the concept into its underlying ideas?
   Is there a sequence of understandings that students need to have?
   What are the related mathematical concepts?

2. **Authentic Experiences**

   In which real-life situations or contexts will students encounter the concept outside of school? Will they see it in science or social studies? In the arts?
   How can I vary these contexts to build a generalized understanding of the concept?
   What version of this situation can I present to start them thinking about the concept?
   What questions can I ask to intrigue them and initiate problem solving?

Figure 6.2

Figure 6.2 *(continued)*

3. **Cognitive Processes in Context**

   How do I scaffold experiences to develop the concept progressively from concrete to abstract? How concretely should I start?

   How can I encourage initial play and exploration with the materials or ideas?

   How can I make the experiences challenging but not overwhelming?

   What questions can I ask or terms can I use to help students visualize or imagine the context, situation, or problem?

4. **Metacognition**

   How will I know/ensure that students are thinking about their own thinking?

   How will I ensure that students are checking to see whether they understand the new material and that "things are working" as they move through a new concept, procedure, or process?

   What self-regulatory questions can I encourage students to ask themselves?

   What feedback can I provide as students move through a new concept?

   How can I model my own metacognitive processes?

5. **Grouping Structures to Encourage the Social Construction of Meaning**

   How can I vary grouping structures: the whole class, small groups of two to five students, individuals?

   How can I enhance small-group discussions so that students develop, refine, and elaborate their thinking?

6. **Language Representations**

   How do I talk about the concept or ask questions to reveal connections or promote reflection?

   How can I model thought processes, strategies, and practices to encourage both cognition and metacognition?

   How can I incorporate reading, writing, speaking, and listening into the activities?

   How can I help students use journals to document, reflect on, and refine their thinking?

7. **Other Representations**

   What manipulatives or physical materials can help students see what is going on?

   Should they draw a picture of objects or of the situation/problem as they imagine it?

   Does the situation contain a sequence of actions that students might perform?

   Should they record information in a list and later organize it into a table?

   What symbols must they understand?

   How does each symbol specifically relate to the situation, objects, or pictures?

8. **Explaining Representations**

   How do I help students communicate (orally/in writing) their solutions and understandings?

   How do I help them move from natural language to more precise mathematical terminology?

   How do I talk about the other mathematical concepts that are related?

(continues)

Figure 6.2 *(continued)*

9. **Patterns**

What patterns (visual, spatial, or numerical) do I want students to see?

What questions can I ask to help them see patterns? What terms or language could I use? What metaphors or analogies could I make?

What connections are important for them to make as we debrief the activity?

What questions do I ask to build bridges, help them make connections?

10. **Problem Posing/Student-Generated Inquiry**

How can I encourage students to generate their own mathematical questions, problems, inquiries, or investigations?

11. **Responsibility**

What student choices and decisions can be built into this activity?

Where do students have control?

What can they be responsible for in their own learning?

How will they know what they have learned?

12. **Understanding Procedures**

What procedures for working with the symbols will be used?

What will I do to help students connect the procedures to their understanding of the concept?

13. **Differentiation**

How do I differentiate the experiences so that students of varying abilities have options and alternatives?

How can I "triple-branch": offer more of the same, make it simpler, make it more challenging?

What kinds of extensions should I provide?

What practice, review, or drill would be valuable?

14. **Assessment (informal/formal, ongoing/summative)**

How will I assess conceptual understanding?

How will I assess thinking processes?

How will I assess students' ability to communicate their mathematical knowledge?

When asking teachers to switch from using the short version to the longer version of these considerations, I emphasize that I do not want them to feel like they need to answer every question that makes up each of the fourteen issues. They are suggestions for *how* to think about the issue being raised.

Big Ideas, Enduring Understandings, and Essential Concepts

To what degree can we help children begin to see mathematics as a coherent whole? It's important to be aware of the hierarchical "web" of ideas surrounding the concept we are teaching and then decide how much of that conceptual structure to build into our activity. The best way to prepare to teach a concept is to work out each of the problems you might use for yourself, preferably in more than one way.

When we break down a concept into its underlying ideas, we may find there are several models that portray the essence of the concept. For example, it is critical for students to understand what multiplication *is* and its relationship to division. As we described in Chapter 2, the traditional way of introducing the group model of multiplication in the fall, skipping over the array model, and then waiting until spring to treat the area model as an application of multiplication is just plain wrongheaded. The three models should be taught in close sequence. Some children may not understand multiplication from the group model but "get it" when they see the array and area models; perhaps they struggle to subitize the quantities clumped together as a group, and the organized structure of the arrays makes it easier to see what is going on.

Authentic Experiences

Students can be enticed into doing some wonderful mathematics by "front-loading" an interesting context and letting the math follow. Then they'll more likely see the math as authentic. Admittedly, motivating students can be a challenge, but all students profit from meaningful contexts. Just because the Common Core Math Standards hold off on statistics and probability concepts until sixth grade should not dissuade us from working with measurement and data concepts that provide great real-world contexts. The real world of science and social studies are filled with opportunities for quantifiable analysis.

Cognitive Processes in Context

Many children have been socialized not to "think" in math class; they wait until we can't bear the silence any longer and give them the procedural steps to follow. I start with a concrete representation that everyone can understand. This is often easiest with geometric concepts in which situations can be physically represented with base-ten blocks, Cuisenaire rods, or pattern blocks. For instance, in working with metric measures of length, the base-ten longs are actually ten centimeters (one decimeter) in length. This fact can be used to approximate traditional measures (i.e., three decimeters or thirty centimeters are very nearly one foot long (1 foot = 30.48 cm). Manipulatives are tools with which to think.

In a world filled with math-anxious or math-phobic people, we should heed the admonition "first do no harm." The worst thing that can happen when we start too concretely with appropriate manipulatives is that some kids get the idea quickly and get a little bored and sassy, in which case we can move on to a less concrete / more abstract representation or challenging question. However, don't mistake difficult or hard for challenging. A task is too difficult if there is no way students can figure it out. Challenging may feel too difficult at first, but the solution is within students' reach if they use good thinking.

When introducing a new manipulative to your students, it is wise to build in some time (five minutes) to let them play and explore what they have. I have found that with most manipulatives I can ask an open-ended question such as: "Tell me about the attributes of these manipulatives. What do you see?" I suggest to teachers that they tell the students that they are doing an "experiential, inductive, exploratory activity" or fancy words to that effect. I don't say "play" unless the children are in second grade or younger. Parents of older children get a trifle annoyed when they hear from their offspring that their math time was spent "playing" with plastic shapes.

A number of years ago, I taught a geometry course to veteran elementary school teachers, who were having a boisterous and delightful time exploring the attributes of pattern blocks. The flimsy partition between my classroom and the neighboring one was unceremoniously parted and the instructor next door, whom I did not know well, poked her head in, a finger raised to her lips, and made a loud shushing noise. We quieted down a bit, and during our break I walked past my neighbor's classroom. She stood at a podium delivering a lecture to students who sat in rows and columns, taking notes. When class was over and I was cleaning up, my neighbor stopped by to apologize for chastising me. She asked what I was teaching and was surprised when I told her. I then asked her what she was teaching. Her reply? "Creative Play"!

Metacognition

The five questions/considerations concerned with metacognition are extremely important. They are best done by a combination of "think-alouds" and direct questions. Hundreds of teachers have told me that KWC is the best metacognitive prompt they have ever found in math. It is part of the overarching strategy of scaffolding learning by asking the right questions that you should write out in advance. Don't try to wing it. Metacognition is too important to leave to chance.

Grouping Structures to Encourage the Social Construction of Meaning

Making meaning, understanding mathematical concepts, and learning in general happen only through social interaction; they are constructed through sharing ideas, expressions, and lives with others. It's a lot easier to teach via lecture: Tell them what they need to know, what steps to follow, what to think. Everyone sits quietly and listens to us talk—like my neighbor teaching Creative Play. Why make trouble by having them work in small groups? The answer is that it gives students more "air time" to talk about how they are conceiving the math ideas they are working with. If we are the only ones who talk, students don't get to process and express the ideas they are developing by sharing with their group.

Many teachers have told me they've tried small groups and they don't work: Kids just jabber about their clothes or the opposite sex. The KWC provides a structure for small-group discussion by encouraging the children to talk about the problem or activity in a particular way. We can practice the process with the whole class, try it out in small groups, and help each student be responsible for internalizing it.

One of the more challenging tasks of small-group work is how to arrange the composition of the groups. Who goes where, how many students are in a group, and for how long? I have tried a variety of ways and talked to many teachers who have had good success. The consensus seems to be that we should have groups of three or four, flexibly arranged for each activity. Whatever attributes you may use to partition the kids, you will run the risk of having other attributes confounding the mixture. For instance, grouping by "ability" by their test scores ignores all the other attributes they have and incurs the problems of tracking kids, such as students who are struggling don't get the stimulation of hearing from those who have grasped the concepts. I'd rather assign them randomly.

My personal interest in grouping is in assigning task roles to each student to perform to make the group effective at finding a solution to the problem. These task roles are not the social roles that are often suggested by group dynamics proponents, such as a "checker" who has to regularly check to make sure everyone in the group understands what the group is doing. But every group member should be aware when understanding has broken down. That is a social responsibility that every member shares.

Task roles are specialized "jobs" that are part of the overall problem-solving task. I have used several different generic task roles that can apply to most problem-solving situations. These include a "reporter" who has the responsibility of taking notes on what the group does; a "recorder" who will record data generated by group on to a recording sheet for the task; a "supplier" in charge of getting the manipulatives or other material needed by the group; and often a task role that is not generic but rather designed for the particular task (e.g., a "sampler" in a probability experiment who must select a sample for the recorder to write down).

I will usually decide on the composition of the groups and have the students and furniture arranged before explaining the task roles and their importance to the overall task. I have a supply of name tags on which I have printed each role in a different color. I write in large letters so that I can see who is appropriately doing the task role assigned by their color.

An excellent resource for how to get the most from kids working in small groups (or *inquiry circles*) is *Comprehension and Collaboration* by Stephanie Harvey and Smokey Daniels (2009). These literacy authors energetically promote an inquiry approach that permeates the entire curriculum. There are three key strands to their version of inquiry teaching and learning:

1. framing school study around questions developed by and shaped by kids as much as possible.

2. handing the brainwork of learning back to the kids . . . no longer . . . delivering all the information, explaining exactly how they should structure their thinking or how they should show what they know.

3. focus on the development of kids' thinking, first, foremost, and always. (2009, 57)

Language Representations

From the first moment we pose a math problem orally or students read about the situation, individual students begin the idiosyncratic process of interpreting what is going on. They create the meaning of the words and imbue them with images, sounds, and emotions that they've experienced or imagined. They sort through these verbal and nonverbal responses and then need to communicate their thinking, also through words, some fairly concrete and descriptive, others more abstract and reflective. Plan on investing the time for a good discussion of what they imagine and express verbally.

Other Representations

What do we need to provide our students so they can enact each of the representational strategies? If we have prepared ourselves by trying various ways to represent the problem, we will be more open to novel approaches, representations, and strategies from the students. Each representation should enable students to see or realize some new aspect of the problem. Each has its own trade-offs that the students should come to understand. If they always choose their favorite single strategy, they would miss out on this valuable feature of representations.

Explaining Their Representations

Feedback to help students explain their thoughts starts while they are trying to understand the problem and continues through debriefing. The nature of the feedback varies depending on where the students are in the conception/implementation/solution process.

Early in the process, asking them open-ended questions related to the KWC helps them move along. Later in the process, questions can focus on content they have missed. Asking them to clarify what they mean by mathematical terms they've used may be appropriate. If they have been using ordinary language to describe a phenomenon that should be addressed with more precise terminology, we can introduce and explain it. While debriefing the activity, you can explain math concepts relating these ideas directly to what they've just experienced and discussed, thereby broadening their web of interconnected concepts.

Patterns

Often students will notice and mention patterns in the course of solving a problem. If they don't, we should ask them to look for patterns—and be prepared to lead them to see these patterns (although they should do the work). Debriefing is our best opportunity to ask *why* the pattern occurs. Their conceptions will be fresh in their minds, and we can tailor our explanations to what they've said about them. It is our teachable moment.

One device that I often use in my preparation is to determine what patterns are there that we can exploit. Most concepts in mathematics are essentially patterns. Therefore, I have suggested to teachers that they rethink the chapter before them in terms of patterns. For example, in a unit on equivalent fractions how would you describe the pattern in $\frac{1}{2}, \frac{2}{3}, \frac{3}{4}, \frac{4}{5}, \frac{5}{6}, \frac{6}{7}$, and so on. What is happening with each successive fraction? Answers may vary!

Problem Posing/Student-Generated Inquiry

We aspire for each student to become a regular problem poser. Our scaffolding should become less necessary over time. However, this can more readily occur after you have given them a focused prompt that they can extend in any way that suits your needs. An example of a focused prompt is the Chocolate Algebra activity described earlier in Chapter 4. After completing it, a class of fourth graders chose two items with different prices, determined a fixed amount of money to spend, and found all the possible ways in which the money could be spent. A more open-ended prompt is described in Chapter 5: third graders read a science curriculum passage about the solar system, listed the questions they had, and decided which of them could be answered using mathematical computations. Students generating their own authentic problem and solving it (or conducting inquiry of their own design) happens so rarely in the traditional math curriculum, yet so many great aspects of mathematics can be incorporated into these kinds of activities.

Responsibility

Our colleagues in reading comprehension have popularized the phrase "gradual release of responsibility" to describe the educator's goal of helping students to assume increasing responsibility for their own learning. We need to consider carefully students' degree of maturity in general (study habits, for example), as well as their mathematical proficiency. Please take time in your planning to think through how you can give students more *choice* of which problem they select. If you use "learning stations," consider keeping them up after everyone has rotated through and allow your students to go back to do extensions of them. Of course, when students pose problems as described earlier, they are also taking responsibility.

Understanding Procedures

Perhaps my repeated emphasis on conceptual understanding has given the impression that I do not value procedures. As a former computer programmer, I know the value of procedures and the necessity for understanding them. How and why procedures work should be an important part of the math curriculum. When students are able to explain the conditions under which a procedure works and why, they demonstrate their understanding of the concepts. Unfortunately, for decades the U.S. math curriculum has valued memorizing procedures more highly than understanding them. Many students (and parents) are unsure which math procedure to use in which situation.

The best preparation for teaching the children why a procedure works is by thoroughly understanding it yourself. The time spent in immersion in the formulas and algebraic structures will pay great dividends. Of course, using good resource books will definitely help as will finding a good math instructor to mentor you. In all candor, I can say that I have had to relearn most of the arithmetic of my elementary school in order to understand and be able to explain to teachers why some procedures work.

For example, the distributive property explains double-digit multiplication procedures using partial products. I have the kids go through five different representations starting with the conception of the multiplication problems as the two sides of a rectangle and one can find its area by multiplying the two sides. The partial products included making the rectangle with base-ten blocks of two different colors, mapping the base-ten blocks onto centimeter-square graph paper, and coloring the rectangle with crayons of the two colors. After debriefing several examples, we then moved to drawing the rectangle on centimeter-square graph paper, as a picture record of several more examples of partial products. Finally, we asked the kids to do some more examples of partial products by drawing the rectangle freehand. In our debriefing we related the each part of the symbolic representation to its corresponding object, picture, or image. See Chapter 3, "Visualization," in *Comprehending Math* (Hyde 2006) for an elaboration of this activity.

Differentiation

The best way to provide meaningful mathematical experiences for students of varying abilities is by encouraging them to work through many representations of a problem. The good news is that differentiation does not mean you have to create thirty different versions of the curriculum. I long ago discovered that I was fortunate if my way of presenting ("pitching") a math problem was right for two-thirds of the class. The remaining one-third either found it impossible or were not challenged by it at all. I now create three versions of each problem, making sure each version has the same mathematical structure but varies in difficulty, usually due to the representation used to communicate the problem.

The lengthy example just given of the multiple representations of partial products illustrates the progressive stripping away of the more concrete aspects of a representation by taking small steps toward a more abstract approach. Everything is interconnected: Some aspect of each previous representation is present in the next. The language description of each representation uses the same terms. Another example is the Chocolate Algebra problems in Chapter 4. Every representation was connected back to the original two items to be bought and to one another. Consequently, students can access the problem through various representations, and once they understand one of them, we can help them translate among the others readily.

Assessment (Informal/Formal, Ongoing/Summative)

Ongoing informal assessment feeds into instructional decisions. Formal and summative assessments validate for the general public, administrators, and boards of education that this kind of mathematic teaching is, in fact, best practice. The official assessments of CCSSM will be implemented in the near future. Meanwhile, educators should be lobbying for local assessments that document students' conceptual understanding of what they have been taught, the kinds of mathematical thinking we expect, and their ability to communicate their mathematical knowledge.

You should use the three considerations to build into the work generated by the students ways for them to demonstrate these three aspects of doing math. In fact, they are taken from the Illinois state test, being the three dimensions on a rubric for extended-response problems. Many teachers have built this rubric into their planning for every activity they do. A good use of your knowledge would be to become involved with those who are creating your own local assessments to have them scored according to the three considerations.

An Example of Using These Considerations

Here's an example of how these planning considerations open up my teaching (a description of this activity may also be found on pages 120–124 of *Comprehending Math* [Hyde 2006]). I was reviewing a videotape of an admired teacher in action, trying to determine whether she valued the same things I did. She held up an opaque bag into which she had placed 10 tiles of 3 different colors. Twenty-eight students were seated around her in a large U. She had each student, in turn, take 1 tile out of the bag, note the color (she kept a running tally on the chalkboard), and return the tile to the bag (a sample of 1, with replacement). From the 28 samples, they were to predict how many tiles of each color tile were in the bag.

I immediately thought about my considerations that asked about grouping the students in various ways. I wondered what would happen if I put the students into groups of three or four and gave each group a bag. I realized that this one simple change greatly alters the dynamics of the problem and opens up a host of mathematical concepts for discussion. I went through my consideration questions and made the following notes.

1. **Concepts**

   - from probability: sample, sample space, replacement, chance
   - from data/statistics: frequency, descriptive vs. inferential statistics
   - from arithmetic: proportion, fractions, percent, decimals, number sense

I reasoned that sixth graders had encountered all these arithmetic concepts before this but they needed to develop the language of probability. I thought that a brief discussion of terms, such as *likely, unlikely, possible, impossible, always, never, probable, improbable, chance* (of rain) would help activate relevant prior knowledge.

2. **Authentic Experiences**

I assumed that this would be tricky because in real-life sampling you rarely, if ever, would have the number of samples be larger than the population. Also most of the real-life contexts are involved in gambling, which I did not want to be accused of promoting. However, I could use casino gambling as the "house" that in the long run always has an edge. Caveat player. Everyone has heard about the weather being unpredictable; that would also be a potentially useful context.

I decided to present the task as a game in which the object was to figure out how many of each color were in the bag. Each group would have to collect raw data from sampling and then report to all what their data were and their prediction of the number of each color in their bag. I had yet to decide the number of colors, how many of which colors, the total number of tiles in the opaque bag, and whether a sample of 1 with replacement would be used.

3. **Cognitive Processes in Context**

I had decided earlier that in the pregame warm-up I would ask students questions using probability language. The game atmosphere would make it sufficiently motivating, playful, and exploratory. The experience would be challenging because in the debriefing I would return to the probability language, asking them questions that would require "probabilistic" thinking known for its rigor.

I would ask the students to look at the data generated by the groups. Do all the groups' bags contain the same number of each color? The data would show some variation among the groups. I would ask the students to decide whether differences occur by chance or because there are different numbers of colored tiles in the bags. How big a difference does there need to be in order to say that the bags are *probably* different? Perhaps 1 bag is different but the others are the same: which bag is *probably* different? How certain are you?

4. Metacognition

I would ask each group to complete a KWC on the task and then use each group's responses to complete a whole-class KWC chart. I envisioned that several times, after students had collected their bag's data and had made predictions of its contents, I would pull the whole class back to debrief what their thinking had been up to now. I would ask each group to explain their reasoning as they went from their data to their prediction.

5. Grouping

I decided to have 8 groups of either 3 or 4. Groups of 3 would have the tasks of reporter and recorder combined. I arranged to use a classroom with a sixth-grade teacher/friend with whom I discussed the composition of his class and his students' prior knowledge. He decided which of his students would be very responsible with the bags to make certain that no one would peek into the bag to determine its contents. He chose 8 students for this role we called the "supplier," the only person allowed to hold the materials.

At this point, I decided to have identical content for the 8 bags, knowing that the sampling would create some differences among the groups' data. Each group would have a sampler whose job was to pull a single tile out of the bag shaken and held aloft by the supplier. The sampler would hold up the tile so that its color could be noted and tallied by the recorder; 25 samples of 1 with replacement would be drawn. I also decided that I would not answer students' questions about the contents of the bags, especially if someone asked if they were all the same. I'd ask them questions about the data from each group.

6, 7, and 8. Representations

The data from each group (given an index card with a unique letter identifying the group) would be recorded for all to see. The data representation would be a tabular record on the board. There would be a lot of data to be considered. I have to decide if they should put up only their data or also include their predictions. I imagine the board would look something like that shown in Figure 6.3.

DATA			
Group	Red	Blue	Yellow
Z			
Y			
X			
W			
V			
U			
T			
S			

PREDICTION			
Group	Red	Blue	Yellow
Z			
Y			
X			
W			
V			
U			
T			
S			

Figure 6.3

A good case could be made for either option: data alone or data and prediction. Their teacher told me that they have done a lot of work with tables. Therefore, I decided to have them send up the reporter once to put both on the board.

During this planning time, I usually ask myself to note where things could get messed up. I noted that I should give each group's recorder a recording sheet with 25 spaces marked on it and the same order of the colors as the board's table. These may prevent a group from collecting 26 or more data points by accident and putting up the data on each color in a different order.

I planned to begin debriefing by having each group report out with the question: How did you go from your data to your prediction? But that raised an important issue. How should I have them represent what they are doing? Their teacher told me that they all should be able to use a variety of calculations (e.g., data of 8, 12, 5 could be $\frac{8}{25}, \frac{12}{25}, \frac{5}{25}$ and divide the numerator by the denominator to calculate a decimal, or they could use proportional reasoning $\frac{8}{25} = \frac{?}{100}$ and multiply each data point by 4 to calculate the percent). Then they have to apply these calculations to the 10 tiles in the bag (e.g., 32%, 48%, and 20%). This means that they would still have to use their number sense to adjust the decimals or the percentages to the bag of 10. Their explanations of how they went from data to prediction will include some reasoning with the frequency data, perhaps not using any procedure, but employing only number sense (e.g., 12 blue is nearly half of 25 so let's call the blue color half of 10 or 5. The other 2 colors would be 3 and 2 or 4 and 1, maybe even 2 and 3). So I asked their teacher if he wanted them to all use the same procedure because I could easily build that into the task. He thought that it would be better to let them use any procedure that was appropriate, so I left it up to the students.

Once they have all moved from the representation on the board to explaining the symbolic representations they used to make a prediction, I will ask them: "How could we make a better prediction? What would you do differently?" I am hoping to get the response that we need more data. Then I could ask: "Why?" or "How would that help?" When they have had sufficient time patiently holding their bags, I would tell them that the contents of the bags are identical. I'll probably need to give them time to express their disbelief because I expect there to be some differences in their data even from identical contents. My retort will always be: "That is what chance will do." However, we could say that we have 8 samples of 25 or 200 samples to use. Therefore we can add up all of the 3 colors and *probably* make a more accurate prediction. It would be great if these ideas came from the kids, but I will be prepared to explain why these might be good ideas.

Having 200 samples of 1 coming from 8 different research teams is probably bad science because there maybe systematic bias in the way they chose the tiles, or shook the bag. Maybe I'll bring that point up. Regardless, 200 is a great number to have as a denominator because one can take half of its numerator as the percent (e.g., $\frac{64}{200} = \frac{32}{100}$ or 32%). Therefore, the students may now use these new percentages for a prediction.

9. Patterns

In my planning I felt that I needed to get a handle on what the actual data might look like. So I did some experimenting with different parameters. I did 25 samples of 1 with replacement with bags of 12 and 4 each of 3 different colors. The data deviated from equating the numbers of the 3 colors somewhat but not enough to make it interesting.

I then experimented with bags of 10 tiles. I tried out sampling on bags of 4,4,2; 5,3,2; 6,3,1; and 5,4,1. The bags that had only 1 tile of a particular color did cause a bit of a problem. When I tried 25 samples of 1, the data occasionally came out with 0 of that single tile. I assumed that kids would be unnecessarily annoyed if that happened to them. This issue caused me to pause and think about allowing the kids to create their own version of this game as an extension activity. But the first encounter with this game ought not to have only 1 tile of any particular color.

I also did not like the results from a 4,4,2 distribution. Very few of my samples of 25 came out 10,10,5. I thought that I wanted the kids to experience success in their predictions in this first version of the game and that having the same number of 2 colors would be an unlikely prediction if the data across the groups were split between these 2 colors. I settled on a 5,3,2 distribution because in the experimenting that I did, most of the time the color with 5 tiles came up the most frequently, and the other 2 colors were definitely rarer.

10. Problem Posing
After they had a basic understanding of the game from one time playing it, I could readily imagine them creating their own similar games with varying parameters.

11. Responsibility
The students will have to behave themselves in dealing with the bag of tiles, multiple task roles, and calculating predictions. Sixth graders should not have a problem with behavior. The use of extensions designed by the students would offer great opportunities for being responsible for their own learning, and they would also be aware of what they had learned. Individual accountability could be assured if I built in that everyone could discuss what they had learned, but each individual must write up a report on the first game and each extension.

12. Understanding Procedures
The symbolic representations of the relative frequencies in the data table would require calculations that must be understood. We could discuss the interpretation of the symbols of $1.00 \geq p \geq 0.00$ in several places (e.g., in the pregame part, discussing how $p = 1.00$ means an event will always occur, and $p = 0.00$ means it will never occur).

13. Differentiation
I decided in my planning that the first time with this game, I would not worry about differentiating the content. In a sense this would be a kind of diagnostic activity to see what students knew about sampling and related concepts. When they create extensions of this game, some of the students may need appropriate scaffolding while others may be able to illustrate a stronger grasp of the concepts and reasoning that must be done.

14. Assessment
As I circulate through the classroom while the groups are determining how to calculate their predictions, I should be able to ascertain what procedure each group is using and to get a sense of which group members have a good grasp of the arithmetic involved. I could tell them that I might call on anyone to explain the calculations, which would mean everyone should be aware of how those calculations were done.

A more formal assessment can be made from the extensions that they do. I'd use a rubric that addressed the three dimensions: conceptual understanding, thinking processes, and communication.

Since my initial reaction to the video of this activity over a decade ago, I have implemented it as I planned it above at least three dozen times. The only change I made was to label the bags with the same letter as the group. This "suggested" to students that the bags were different. I was not trying to trick them but rather to let them assume the contents were different to allow for a very rich discussion of the key inferential questions raised by the sampling data.

In about 40 times that I have done this activity, every single time there was at least 1 group whose data were very different from the others. And on one occasion a group pulled out 1 of the 2 yellow tiles or cubes 15 times, phenomenally unlikely to happen! As if to drive the major points of sampling home, the other groups that day pulled out fewer than 20% yellow. However, when adding the results from all groups the yellow total was close to the 20% expected. On nearly every occasion the summing of data across the 8 groups approximates the 50%, 30%, 20% that we would predict.

Summing Up

My excitement at writing this book was fueled by the opportunity for some wonderful teachers, whom I have come to know, to share what they do. Equally important is to share what they believe about mathematics, teaching, and children. Even though I am old enough to be their father, a generation away in time, in spirit we are cut from the same cloth, and I count them among my dearest friends.

Our hope is that as you have read this book you will have been surprised by many things and thrilled at many others. Surprised by what we have asked kids to do, things seemingly too difficult for regular kids. Thrilled because we validated what you have been doing without much support.

We have unabashedly advocated for greater attention to cognitive processes as a critically important part of the curriculum. How children come to understand and even love mathematics is as important as which math concepts we try to teach them. In so doing, the cognition that undergirds the understanding of mathematics often mirrors that by which children understand ideas in reading and language arts. It is foolish to make walls of demarcation between them. Metacognition deserves renewed attention in mathematics. Hundreds of teachers have found real success in doing the KWL in reading and the KWC in math. It is one of the easiest ways to start off the school year.

We have encouraged you to explore what limits you from creating real-world, authentic problem solving for kids. Push the envelope! If students are going to be faced with problems that can be best understood mathematically in their adult lives, should we spoon-feed them until their eighteenth birthdays? If math modeling represents the best kind of mathematics activity we have to offer children, why wait?

We can do a much better job with building so-called skills into modeling activities than we do now working the numbers without a context. Even though it is a rare child who enjoys drill and practice, when I present an intriguing context for students to explore (as in Chocolate Algebra), they are excited by the context and willingly crunch the numbers with more zeal and accuracy than ever before.

Appendix

Resources for Teaching Mathematics

Books by Martin Gardner taken from his Mathematical Games column in *Scientific American* and a few others of the same orientation. Check local libraries.

The Scientific American Book of Mathematical Puzzles and Diversions. 1959. New York: Simon and Schuster.

The 2nd Scientific American Book of Mathematical Puzzles and Diversions. 1961. New York: Simon and Schuster.

Martin Gardner's New Mathematical Diversions from Scientific American. 1966. New York: Simon and Schuster.

The Unexpected Hanging and Other Mathematical Diversions. 1969. New York: Simon and Schuster.

Martin Gardner's Sixth Book of Mathematical Games from Scientific American. 1971. New York: Simon and Schuster.

Mathematical Carnival. 1977. New York: Vintage Books.

Mathematical Circus. 1981. New York: Vintage Books.

Wheels, Life, and Other Mathematical Amusements. 1983. New York: W. H. Freeman and Co.

Penrose Tiles to Trapdoor Ciphers. 1989. New York: W. H. Freeman and Co.

Fractal Music, Hypercards, and More . . . 1992. New York: W. H. Freeman and Co.

The Last Recreations. 1997. New York: Springer-Verlag.

Berlekamp, E., and T. Rodgers, eds. 1999. *The Mathemagician and Pied Puzzler: A Collection in Tribute to Martin Gardner*. Natick, MA: A K Peters.

COMAP. 2009. *For All Practical Purposes: Mathematical Literacy in Today's World*. 8th ed. New York: W. H. Freeman and Co.

Golomb, S. 1994. *Polyominoes*. 2d ed. Princeton NJ: Princeton University Press.

Jacobs, H. 1994. *Mathematics: A Human Endeavor*. 3d ed. New York: W. H. Freeman and Co.

Peterson, I. 1988. *The Mathematical Tourist: Snapshots of Modern Mathematics*. New York: W. H. Freeman and Co.

References

Andrews, A., and L. Huber. n.d. *Ten Frames Number Deck*. Fort Atkinson, WI: NASCO.

Ausubel, D. 1978. *Educational Psychology: A Cognitive View*. 2d ed. New York: Holt, Rinehart, and Winston.

Bickmore-Brand, J., ed. 1990. *Language in Mathematics*. Portsmouth, NH: Heinemann.

Blachowicz, C., and D. Ogle. 2001. *Reading Comprehension: Strategies for Independent Learners*. New York: Guilford.

Bransford, J., A. Brown, and R. Cocking, eds. 2000. *How People Learn: Brain, Mind, Experience, and School*. Expanded ed. Washington, DC: National Research Council (NRC) and National Academy Press.

Brown, S., and M. Walter. 1990. *The Art of Problem Posing*. 2d ed. Mahwah, NJ: Lawrence Erlbaum Associates.

Brown, S., and M. Walter, eds. 1993. *Problem Posing: Reflections and Applications*. East Sussex, UK: Psychology Press.

Common Core State Standards Initiative. 2011. *Common Core State Standards for Mathematics*. www.corestandards.org

Devlin, K. 2000. *The Math Gene: How Mathematical Thinking Evolved and Why Numbers Are Like Gossip*. New York: Basic Books.

Dienes, Z. 1960. *Building Up Mathematics*. London: Hutchinson Educational Ltd.

Donovan, M., and J. Bransford, eds. 2005. *How Students Learn: History, Mathematics, and Science in the Classroom*. Washington, DC: National Research Council (NRC) and National Academy Press.

Fauconnier, G., and M. Turner. 2002. *The Way We Think: Conceptual Blending and the Mind's Hidden Complexities*. New York: Basic Books.

Fosnot, C., and W. Uittenbogaard. 2006. *Minilessons for Early Addition and Subtraction: A Yearlong Resource*. Portsmouth, NH: Heinemann.

Gawned, S. 1990. "The Emerging Model of the Language of Mathematics." In *Language in Mathematics*, edited by J. Bickmore-Brand, 27–42. Portsmouth, NH: Heinemann.

Gerofsky, S. 2004. *A Man Left Albuquerque Heading East: Word Problems as Genre in Mathematics Education.* New York: Peter Lang.

Greenes, C., et al. 1989. *Amazing Facts and Real Problems.* Palo Alto, CA: Creative Publications.

Harvey, S., and A. Goudvis. 2007. *Strategies That Work: Teaching Comprehension for Understanding and Engagement.* 2d ed. Portland, ME: Stenhouse.

Harvey, S., and H. Daniels. 2009. *Comprehension and Collaboration: Inquiry Circles in Action.* Portsmouth, NH: Heinemann.

Hiebert, J., R. Gallimore, H. Garnier, K. Givvin, H. Hollingsworth, A. Chui, D. Wearne, M. Smith, N. Kersting, A. Manaster, E. Tseng, W. Etterbeek, C. Manaster, P. Gonzales, and J. Stigler. 2003. *Teaching Mathematics in Seven Countries: Results from the TIMSS 1999 Video Study.* Washington, DC: U.S. Department of Education, National Center for Educational Statistics.

Hyde, A. 2006. *Comprehending Math: Adapting Reading Strategies to Teach Mathematics K–6.* Portsmouth, NH: Heinemann.

Hyde, A., and M. Bizar. 1989. *Thinking in Context: Teaching Cognitive Processes Across the Elementary School Curriculum.* New York: Longman.

Hyde, A., with S. Friedlander, C. Heck, and L. Pittner. 2009. *Understanding Middle School Math.* Portsmouth, NH: Heinemann.

Keene, E. O. 2008. *To Understand: New Horizons in Reading Comprehension.* Portsmouth, NH: Heinemann.

Keene, E. O., and S. Zimmermann. 2007. *Mosaic of Thought: The Power of Comprehension Instruction.* 2d ed. Portsmouth, NH: Heinemann.

Lakoff, G., and R. E. Nuñez. 2000. *Where Mathematics Comes From: How the Embodied Mind Brings Mathematics into Being.* New York: Basic Books.

Lehrer, R., and L. Schauble, eds. 2002. *Investigating Real Data in the Classroom: Expanding Children's Understanding of Math and Science.* New York: Teachers College Press.

Lesh R., and H. M. Doerr. 2003a. "Foundations of a Models and Modeling Perspective on Mathematics Teaching, Learning, and Problem Solving." In *Beyond Constructivism: Models and Modeling Perspectives on Mathematics Problem Solving, Learning, and Teaching,* edited by R. Lesh and H. M. Doerr, 3–34. Mahwah, NJ: Lawrence Erlbaum Associates.

Lesh, R., and H. M. Doerr, eds. 2003b. *Beyond Constructivism: Models and Modeling Perspectives on Mathematics Problem Solving, Learning, and Teaching.* Mahwah, NJ, Lawrence Erlbaum Associates.

Lesh, R., and J. Zawojewski. 2006. "Problem Solving and Modeling." In *The Handbook for Research on Mathematics Education*, edited by F. Lester, 763–804. Reston, VA: National Council of Teachers of Mathematics.

Lesh, R., K. Cramer, H. Doerr, T. Post, and J. Zawojewski. 2003. "Model Development Sequences." In *Beyond Constructivism: Models and Modeling Perspectives on Mathematics Problem Solving, Learning, and Teaching*, edited by R. Lesh and H. M. Doerr, 35–58. Mahwah, NJ: Lawrence Erlbaum Associates.

Lester, F., and P. Kehle. 2003."From Problem Solving to Modeling: The Evolution of Thinking About Research on Complex Mathematical Activity." In *Beyond Constructivism: Models and Modeling Perspectives on Mathematics Problem Solving, Learning, and Teaching*, edited by R. Lesh and H. Doerr, 501–18. Mahwah, NJ: Lawrence Erlbaum Associates.

Miura, I. 1987. "Asian Languages Aid Mathematics Skills." *Science News* 132 (Sept. 19).

———. 2001. "The Influence of Language on Mathematical Representations." In *The Roles of Representation in School Mathematics*, edited by A. Cuoco, 53–62. Reston, VA: National Council of Teachers of Mathematics.

National Council of Teachers of Mathematics. 1989. *Curriculum and Evaluation Standards for School Mathematics*. Reston, VA: National Council of Teachers of Mathematics.

———. 2000. *Principles and Standards for School Mathematics*. Reston, VA: National Council of Teachers of Mathematics.

National Research Council (NRC). 2001. *Adding It Up: Helping Children Learn Mathematics*. Washington, DC: National Academy Press.

Steen, L. A., ed. 1990. *On the Shoulders of Giants: New Approaches to Numeracy*. Washington, DC: National Academy Press.

Stigler, J., and J. Hiebert. 2004. "Improving Mathematics Teaching." *Educational Leadership* 61 (5): 12–17.

Von Glasersfeld, E. 2003. Review of "Beyond Constructivism." In *Zentralblatt für Didaktik der Mathematik* 35 (6): 3.

Wright, R., J. Martland, and A. Stafford. 2006. *Early Numeracy: Assessment for Teaching and Intervention*. 2d ed. London: Paul Chapman Publishing.

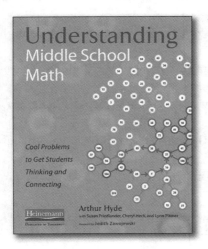